英语导学拓展模块

主　编　郭建成　吕立茹

北京理工大学出版社
BEIJING INSTITUTE OF TECHNOLOGY PRESS

版权专有　侵权必究

图书在版编目（CIP）数据

英语导学拓展模块 / 郭建成，吕立茹主编 . — 北京：北京理工大学出版社，2020.7 重印

ISBN 978-7-5682-6151-7

Ⅰ . ①英… Ⅱ . ①郭… ②吕… Ⅲ . ①英语课 – 中等专业学校 – 教学参考资料 Ⅳ . ① G634.413

中国版本图书馆 CIP 数据核字（2018）第 190441 号

出版发行 / 北京理工大学出版社有限责任公司
社　　址 / 北京市海淀区中关村南大街 5 号
邮　　编 / 100081
电　　话 /（010）68914775（总编室）
　　　　　（010）82562903（教材售后服务热线）
　　　　　（010）68948351（其他图书服务热线）
网　　址 / http：//www.bitpress.com.cn
经　　销 / 全国各地新华书店
印　　刷 / 定州市新华印刷有限公司
开　　本 / 787 毫米 × 1092 毫米　1/16
印　　张 / 9.5　　　　　　　　　　　　　　　责任编辑 / 梁铜华
字　　数 / 196 千字　　　　　　　　　　　　　文案编辑 / 梁铜华
版　　次 / 2020 年 7 月第 1 版第 3 次印刷　　　责任校对 / 周瑞红
定　　价 / 29.00 元　　　　　　　　　　　　　责任印制 / 边心超

图书出现印装质量问题，请拨打售后服务热线，本社负责调换

中等职业教育创优导航文化素养提升系列丛书

编写委员会

主　任　　张志增

委　员　　（按首字汉字笔画排序）

　　　　　于春红　韦玉海　陈宝忠

　　　　　张秀魁　张剑锋　张健智

　　　　　郝玉华　郭建成　黄书林

本书编写组

主　编　　郭建成　吕立茹

副主编　　崔桂芬　宋玉霞

参　编　　张　丽　倪冉肖

　　本书是根据教育部颁发的《中等职业学校英语教学大纲》,以教育部指定的中等职业教育课程改革国家规划新教材《英语基础模块上册》《英语基础模块下册》《英语拓展模块》为主要参考教材,结合中等职业学校就业与升学的实际情况而编写的。

　　本书的指导思想是,在掌握单词、词汇的基础上,强化了基础知识、基本能力的训练;在掌握知识重点、难点的前提下,在知识运用的灵活性上做了一些尝试;坚持夯实基础、提高能力的原则,内容更加紧扣最新教学大纲,做到了知识点全面、知识系统,试题典型,面向全体学生,难易适中,很好地满足了职业学校的学生参加对口升学考试的需求。

　　本书分为单元基础知识闯关小测验、单元综合练习、阶段测试题、期中综合测试题、期末综合测试题,以及综合模拟试题。

　　单元基础知识闯关小测验考查每单元的重点词汇、短语的用法。单元综合练习包括语音知识和单选,其中单选题中重点考查本单元所涉及的语法知识;完形和阅读理解题各一篇,单词匹配题、词形变换题、单词拼写题、改错题重现本单元的重点词汇、语法,能有效地达到举一反三、灵活运用所学知识点的目的。每学完三个单元后,我们精心准备了阶段测试题,阶段测试题和高考题型、题量完全一致。

　　我们本着"注重基础,突出运用,精选内容,强化训练,提高分数"的原则,力争做到"由浅入深、循序渐进",符合中等职业学校学生的认知特点和接受能力。本书可作为中等职业学校教师的复习教学用书,也可作为一、二年级学生日常学习参考,对于参加对口升学的毕业班学生来说同样适用。

本书的作者均是来自教学一线,有多年教学经验的教师。但由于水平有限,错误和不足之处在所难免,恳请各位老师、同学及各位读者批评指正。

编　者

Unit 1 Social Communication
　　单元基础知识闯关小测验 ………… 1
　　单元综合练习 ………… 2
Unit 2 Making Choices in Life
　　单元基础知识闯关小测验 ………… 8
　　单元综合练习 ………… 9
阶段测试题（Unit 1～Unit 2）………… 15
　　第一部分　英语知识运用 ………… 15
　　第二部分　篇章与词汇理解 ………… 18
　　第三部分　语言技能运用 ………… 23
Unit 3 Fashion
　　单元基础知识闯关小测验 ………… 25
　　单元综合练习 ………… 26
Unit 4 Colors and Mood
　　单元基础知识闯关小测验 ………… 32
　　单元综合练习 ………… 33
阶段测试题（Unit 3～Unit 4）………… 39
　　第一部分　英语知识运用 ………… 39
　　第二部分　篇章与词汇理解 ………… 42
　　第三部分　语言技能运用 ………… 47
Unit 5 Good Manners
　　单元基础知识闯关小测验 ………… 49
　　单元综合练习 ………… 50

Unit 6 Chinese Heritage
    单元基础知识闯关小测验 …………………… 56
    单元综合练习 ………………………………… 57
阶段测试题（Unit 5～Unit 6）………………… 63
    第一部分　英语知识运用 …………………… 63
    第二部分　篇章与词汇理解 ………………… 66
    第三部分　语言技能运用 …………………… 71
期中综合测试题 ………………………………… 73
    第一部分　英语知识运用 …………………… 73
    第二部分　篇章与词汇理解 ………………… 76
    第三部分　语言技能运用 …………………… 81
期末综合测试题 ………………………………… 83
    第一部分　英语知识运用 …………………… 83
    第二部分　篇章与词汇理解 ………………… 86
    第三部分　语言技能运用 …………………… 91
综合模拟试题（一）……………………………… 93
    第一部分　英语知识运用 …………………… 93
    第二部分　篇章与词汇理解 ………………… 96
    第三部分　语言技能运用 ………………… 101
综合模拟试题（二）……………………………… 103
    第一部分　英语知识运用 ………………… 103
    第二部分　篇章与词汇理解 ………………… 106
    第三部分　语言技能运用 ………………… 112
综合模拟试题（三）……………………………… 114
    第一部分　英语知识运用 ………………… 114
    第二部分　篇章与词汇理解 ………………… 117
    第三部分　语言技能运用 ………………… 122
综合模拟试题（四）……………………………… 124
    第一部分　英语知识运用 ………………… 124
    第二部分　篇章与词汇理解 ………………… 127
    第三部分　语言技能运用 ………………… 131
参考答案 ………………………………………… 133

Unit 1 Social Communication

单元基础知识闯关小测验

★★★

I. 汉译英。

1. 对……宽容_____
2. 在……方面(没有)麻烦_____
3. 生……的气_____
4. 忽视,遗忘_____
5. 假装要做某事_____
6. 与……交谈_____
7. 转而谈论_____
8. 向某人解释_____

II. 词形变换。

1. tolerant _____（名词）
2. explain _____（名词）
3. politely _____（形容词）
4. lost _____（名词）
5. understand _____（反义词）
6. face _____（形容词）

III. 用括号内所给词的适当形式填空。

1. The _____ (respond) to "Thank you" is "You are welcome."
2. They quarreled because they _____ (understand) each other.
3. _____ (Children) as he is, he knows a lot.
4. Don't leave the boy _____ (stand) all the time.
5. He was angry because he felt _____ (leave) out.
6. He was _____ (annoy) with his wife because the dinner was badly cooked.

单元综合练习

★★★

第一节 语音知识：从 A、B、C、D 四个选项中找出其画线部分与所给单词画线部分读音相同的选项。

( ) 1. t<u>a</u>ste   A. r<u>a</u>ther   B. h<u>a</u>ndshake   C. f<u>a</u>cial   D. <u>a</u>dmit

( ) 2. e<u>x</u>plain   A. e<u>x</u>ample   B. e<u>x</u>it   C. e<u>x</u>cuse   D. e<u>x</u>pert

( ) 3. r<u>u</u>de   A. s<u>u</u>ggest   B. j<u>u</u>mp   C. incl<u>u</u>de   D. <u>u</u>seful

( ) 4. l<u>ea</u>ve   A. br<u>ea</u>d   B. br<u>ea</u>k   C. ar<u>ea</u>   D. m<u>ea</u>n

( ) 5. ra<u>th</u>er   A. <u>th</u>ank   B. ga<u>th</u>er   C. <u>th</u>ick   D. <u>th</u>ink

第二节 词汇与语法知识：从 A、B、C、D 四个选项中选出可以填入空白处的最佳选项。

( ) 1. I really can't be tolerant _____ what they said just now.
    A. for   B. of   C. with   D. in

( ) 2. The student pretended _____ what the teacher said in class.
    A. understand   B. understanding
    C. to understand   D. of understanding

( ) 3. What is the man annoyed _____ , _____ his wife?
    A. at, at   B. at, with   C. in, with   D. on, with

( ) 4. It is quite rude _____ a foreigner in your native language.
    A. talk with   B. talk about   C. to talk with   D. to talk about

( ) 5. More and more people die _____ air pollution every year.
    A. because   B. since   C. for   D. because of

( ) 6. _____ walks around in such a heavy rain will catch a cold.
    A. No matter who   B. No matter what
    C. Whoever   D. Whatever

( ) 7. _____ happens, don't be surprised.
    A. No matter what   B. Not matter what
    C. Whatever   D. A and C

( ) 8. He admitted _____ the old man's wallet.
    A. steal   B. stole   C. stolen   D. stealing

(　　)9. Don't touch my writing table, leave it _____ it is.

　　A. like　　　　B. so　　　　　C. as　　　　　D. for

(　　)10. _____ you have come, you may stay here for some days.

　　A. Now that　　B. As for　　　C. As long as　　D. As far as

(　　)11. —How is everything with you?

　　—_____.

　　A. How are you　　　　　　　B. I'm very well

　　C. I'm ill　　　　　　　　　D. Same as usual

(　　)12. Tom explains everything that happened just now _____ me.

　　A. for　　　　B. to　　　　　C. at　　　　　D. in

(　　)13. The man left _____ a letter in his e-mail so that he made a mistake.

　　A. for　　　　B. to　　　　　C. in　　　　　D. out

(　　)14. They left Beijing _____ Shanghai.

　　A. for　　　　B. in　　　　　C. to　　　　　D. at

(　　)15. _____ should you say when someone sneezes?

　　A. What　　　B. Who　　　　C. How　　　　D. Why

(　　)16. _____ a few more polite expression, and you'll be ready to face the world of Americans.

　　A. Learning　　B. To learn　　C. Learned　　　D. Learn

(　　)17. He is _____ to drive a car.

　　A. young enough　B. enough young　C. old enough　D. enough old

(　　)18. I will call you if he _____ here tomorrow.

　　A. come　　　B. comes　　　C. will come　　D. came

(　　)19. He asked me if the writer _____ tomorrow.

　　A. comes　　　B. will come　　C. came　　　　D. would come

(　　)20. The woman remembered _____ down the right address but she couldn't find the paper.

　　A. write　　　B. to write　　C. writing　　　D. written

第三节　完形填空：阅读下面的短文，从所给的 A、B、C、D 四个选项中选出最佳的答案。

Yesterday I read a report on a charity show in a local newspaper. The aim of the show was to __1__ money for the poor children. In the poor areas, some children were out of school __2__ their parents couldn't pay for their education.

To my surprise, many pop stars __3__ the charity show, such as Andy Liu, Jay, Faye Wang and Kitty Chen. The stars didn't ask for any payment. They did it for long! There were a lot of performances __4__ singing and dancing. The audience (观众) were so __5__ that they clapped their hands from time to time. Of course, the show was __6__.

All the people followed the stars' example. A great number of people __7__ their money to the show. Both the ticket money and the donated money were soon sent to the poor areas and some of the poor children could get back to school.

Now many charity shows __8__ on our country, not only to support the education in poor areas, but also to help people in trouble. As the Chinese saying goes, "All the others will come to one's rescue (援助) __9__ one is in trouble." I __10__ the whole world will become better and better if each of us gives charity to others.

( )1. A. pay   B. raise   C. spend   D. cost
( )2. A. and   B. so   C. because   D. because of
( )3. A. took part in   B. joined   C. got to   D. had
( )4. A. like   B. as   C. of   D. for
( )5. A. exciting   B. excited   C. sad   D. surprised
( )6. A. a success   B. succeeded   C. successes   D. successful
( )7. A. donated   B. brought   C. collected   D. took
( )8. A. hold   B. are holding   C. are held   D. will be held
( )9. A. because   B. than   C. before   D. when
( )10. A. like   B. wish   C. believe   D. want

第四节 阅读理解:阅读下列短文,从每题所给 A、B、C、D 四个选项中,选出最恰当的答案。

The United States of America is the fourth largest country in the world (after Russia, Canada and China). It takes up the southern part of North America and stretches from the Pacific Ocean to the Atlantic Ocean. It also includes Alaska in the north and Hawaii in the Pacific Ocean. The total area of the country is about nine and a half million square kilometers. The USA borders on Canada in the north and on Mexico in the south. It also has a sea border with Russia.

The USA is made up of 50 states and the District of Columbia, a special federal area where the capital of the country, Washington, is situated. The population of the country is more than 270 million.

If we look at the map of the USA, we can see lowlands and mountains. The highest mountains are the Rocky Mountains, the Cordillera and the Sierra Nevada. The highest peak is Mount Mckinley which is located in Alaska.

America's largest rivers are the Mississippi, the Missouri, the Rio Grande and the Columbia. The Great Lakes on the border with Canada are the largest and deepest in the USA.

The climate of the country varies greatly. The coldest regions are in the north. The climate of Alaska is very cold. The climate of the central part is continental. The south has a subtropical climate. Hot winds blowing from the Gulf of Mexico often bring typhoons. The climate along the Pacific coast is much warmer than that of the Atlantic coast.

The largest cities are: New York, Los Angeles, Chicago, Philadelphia, Detroit, San Francisco, Washington and others.

( )1. The second largest country in the world is _____.
　A. China　　　B. Canada　　　C. Russia　　　D. the USA

( )2. The total area of the USA is about _____ square kilometers.
　A. 9,500,000　　B. 9,300,000　　C. 9,100,000　　D. 9,450,000

( )3. The highest peak in the USA is _____.
　A. the Rocky Mountain　　　B. the Cordillera
　C. The Sierra Nevada　　　　D. Mount Mckinley

( )4. The typhoons are often from _____.
　A. The Pacific coast　　　　B. the Atlantic coast
　C. The Gulf of Mexico　　　 D. Alaska

( )5. The coldest region of the USA is in _____.
　A. Alaska　　　　　　　　　B. Hawaii
　C. New York　　　　　　　　D. Los Angeles

第五节 词义搭配:从(B)栏中选出(A)栏单词的正确解释。

(A)   (B)

(　　)1. pretend   A. make sb. rather angry

(　　)2. handshake   B. impolite

(　　)3. annoyed   C. give an appearance of sth. that is not true

(　　)4. native   D. greeting given by grasping a person's hand

(　　)5. rude   E. person born in a place or a country

第六节 补全对话:根据对话内容,从对话后的选项中选出能填入空白处的最佳选项。

Li:Hi,Xiao Wang. Is that you?　__1__

Wang:Right! How is everything with you?

Li:Same as usual. I'm still studying in the vocational school.　__2__

Wang:I'm now working at a car repair workshop.

Li:　__3__

Wang:Pretty good. I can support myself now. Every month I can also send some money back home.

Li:That's great!

Wang:　__4__

Li:Is that OK?

Wang:Don't worry! The dinner is on me.

Li:　__5__

Wang:Don't mention it. Let's go!

> A. That's really very kind of you.
> B. I haven't seen you for ages.
> C. How have you been?
> D. What about you?
> E. By the way,why don't we have dinner together?

第七节 单词拼写。

1. If you _____(不同意) with my idea, we can ask our teacher for some advice.

2. Can you _____(解释) why you were absent?

3. After answering the question, he suddenly _____ (转换) to another question.

4. The polite response to a _____ (赞美) about your looks is "Thank you."

5. He _____ (误解) what I said just now.

第八节　词形变换。

1. She has no _____ (difficult) reading the novel in a week.

2. We should treat the old _____ (polite).

3. I think we should cherish our _____ (friend).

4. Do you think whether I am _____ (suit) for the job?

5. By _____ (mean) of doing exercises every day, the old man recovered quickly.

第九节　改错：从 A、B、C、D 四个画线处找出一处错误的选项填入括号内，并在横线上写出正确答案。

1. The woman is so old that she wants to send to her children.
　　　　　　　A　　　　　　　B　　　C　　D

2. What a nice weather! Let's have a picnic in the park.
　　A　　B　　　　　C　　　　　　D

3. Don't leave the boy to stand in the sun
　　A　　B　　　　C　　　D

4. Remember calling me as soon as you get there.
　　　A　　　B　　　C　　　　D

5. If you must explain something to a non-English speaker, you'll tell them so that
　　　　　　　A　　　　　　　B
　　they don't feel leave out.
　　　　C　　　D

1. (　　) 应为_____   2. (　　) 应为_____

3. (　　) 应为_____   4. (　　) 应为_____

5. (　　) 应为_____

第十节　作文。

假设你是北京职业学校的一名学生李明，得知某英文报刊招聘兼职记者，你有意应聘，请按下列要点写一封自荐信：

1. 表示感兴趣。

2. 说明优势：知识面、英语水平、合作精神。

Unit 2 Making Choices in Life

单元基础知识闯关小测验

★★★

I. 汉译英。

1. 求人帮助_____   2. 陷入某情况_____
3. 多亏、由于_____   4. 坚持、坚决认为_____
5. 环顾四周_____   6. 容光焕发_____
7. 为……付钱_____   8. 与……争论_____

II. 词形变换。

1. choose _____（名词）   2. succeed _____（名词）
3. honest _____（副词）   4. empty _____（反义词）
5. stomach _____（复数）   6. attract _____（形容词）

III. 用括号内所给词的适当形式填空。

1. Don't feel _____ (depress) even if you are not successful.
2. An ant has two _____ (stomach).
3. Thanks to the doctor's _____ (treat), he was saved.
4. Either you or I _____ (be) wrong.
5. Tom and Mary succeeded in _____ (pass) the exam last week.
6. We should earn money _____ (honest).

单元综合练习

第一节 语音知识：从 A、B、C、D 四个选项中找出其画线部分与所给单词画线部分读音相同的选项。

( )1. h<u>a</u>te   A. sh<u>a</u>pe   B. f<u>a</u>ll   C. m<u>a</u>nager   D. g<u>a</u>ther

( )2. m<u>oo</u>d   A. <u>ou</u>tlook   B. f<u>oo</u>t   C. c<u>oo</u>l   D. bl<u>oo</u>d

( )3. <u>g</u>eneral   A. a<u>g</u>ree   B. <u>g</u>ladly   C. en<u>g</u>age   D. ar<u>g</u>ue

( )4. depress<u>ed</u>   A. play<u>ed</u>   B. watch<u>ed</u>   C. want<u>ed</u>   D. succeed<u>ed</u>

( )5. pr<u>i</u>ce   A. m<u>i</u>ddle-aged   B. <u>i</u>nsist   C. v<u>i</u>ctim   D. pol<u>i</u>te

第二节 词汇与语法知识：从 A、B、C、D 四个选项中选出可以填入空白处的最佳选项。

( )1. He _____ a lazy man when he was young.
    A. used to being   B. was used to be   C. used to be   D. was to

( )2. He insisted _____ here.
    A. stay   B. on stay   C. in staying   D. on staying

( )3. When I came in, I found a _____ dog _____ under the desk.
    A. die, lie   B. dead, lying   C. dying, lied   D. died, to lie

( )4. We were _____ by the _____ movie.
    A. moving, moved   B. moving, moving
    C. moved, moving   D. moved, moved

( )5. Mike was _____ guy you love to hate.
    A. the kind   B. a kind   C. the kind of   D. the kinds

( )6. Please remember _____ the lights when you leave.
    A. to turn on   B. to turn off   C. turning on   D. turning off

( )7. This pair of shoes _____ in fashion now.
    A. is   B. are   C. was   D. were

( )8. He is a tireless person, and he is always _____ a good mood.
    A. on   B. in   C. for   D. at

( )9. Mary used to work 12 hours, _____?
    A. usedn't she   B. didn't Mary   C. used she   D. did she

( )10. Five yuan _____ enough for me to buy a pen.
   A. is   B. are   C. was   D. were

( )11. My teacher told me _____ in time.
   A. what to finish it   B. how to finish it
   C. what did finish it   D. how did finish it

( )12. The boy would rather stay with his small dog, _____ he?
   A. would   B. would rather not
   C. would rather   D. wouldn't

( )13. Why not choose _____ that we love and live happily?
   A. another   B. the one   C. the other   D. others

( )14. He _____ much money, but he failed.
   A. tries to make   B. managed to make
   C. tried to make   D. manages to make

( )15. We should take a positive outlook _____ losing hope.
   A. instead   B. take the place of
   C. take our places of   D. instead of

( )16. He promised _____ his son to go hiking.
   A. taking   B. take   C. took   D. to take

( )17. The kids were _____ breath after running.
   A. in   B. out of   C. from   D. under

( )18. I have _____ in writing the novel since last month.
   A. engaged   B. been taken C. been engaged D. taken

( )19. His face _____ because of the good news.
   A. lights up   B. lit up   C. lighted on   D. was lit up

( )20. My suggestion is that a few more doctors _____ to the country.
   A. be sent   B. sent   C. have sent   D. should send

第三节　完形填空：阅读下面的短文，从所给的 A、B、C、D 四个选项中选出最佳的答案。

Tom and Fred were talking about the year 2050.

"What will the world be like in   1   year 2050?" asked Tom.

"I don't know," said Fred. "What do you think?"

Unit 2　Making Choices in Life

"Well, no one knows. But it is __2__ to guess," said Tom. "In the year 2050 everybody will __3__ a pocket (袖珍) computer. The computer will give people the __4__ to all their problems. We shall all have telephones in our pockets, __5__ . And we'll be able to talk to our friends all over the world. Perhaps we'll be able to see them __6__ the same time. Machines will do __7__ of the work, and people will have more __8__ . Perhaps they will work only two __9__ three days a week. They will be able to fly to the moon by spaceship and spend their holidays there."

"I'm very glad to hear that. I hope to fly to the moon. And I hope I'll be able to live in the sea," said Fred. "Won't that be interesting? Just __10__ a fish."

(　　)1. A. /　　　　B. a　　　　C. an　　　　D. the
(　　)2. A. pleased　B. no use　　C. interesting　D. unusual
(　　)3. A. carry　　B. bring　　C. give　　　D. send
(　　)4. A. news　　B. ways　　C. things　　D. answers
(　　)5. A. either　　B. again　　C. too　　　D. also
(　　)6. A. in　　　B. at　　　C. for　　　D. with
(　　)7. A. many　　B. most　　C. lot　　　D. some
(　　)8. A. work　　B. duty　　C. holidays　　D. times
(　　)9. A. and　　B. or　　　C. with　　　D. along
(　　)10. A. as　　　B. alike　　C. like　　　D. seem

第四节　阅读理解：阅读下列短文，从每题所给 A、B、C、D 四个选项中，选出最恰当的答案。

Americans with small families own a small car or a large one. If both parents are working, they usually have two cars. When the family is large, one of the cars is sold and they will buy a van(住房汽车).

A small car can hold four persons and a large car can hold six persons, but it is very crowded. A van holds seven persons easily, so a family with three children could ask their grandparents to go on a holiday travel. They could all travel together.

Mr Hagen and his wife had a third child last year. This made them sell a second car and buy a van. Their sixth and seventh seats are used to put other things, for a family of five must carry many suitcases when they travel. When they arrive at their grandparents' home, the suitcases are brought into the two seats and then carry the

grandparents.

Americans call vans motor homes. A motor home is always used for holidays. When a family are traveling to the mountains or to the seaside, they can live in their motor home for a few days or weeks. All the members of a big family can enjoy a happier life when they are traveling together. That is why motor homes have become very popular. In America there are many parks for motor homes.

( )1. From the passage, a van is also called _____.

　　A. a motor car   B. a motorbike   C. a big truck   D. a motor home

( )2. Before Mr Hagen and his wife bought a van, they _____.

　　A. sold their second car　　　B. moved to their grandparents' house

　　C. built a new place for a van　　D. sold their old house

( )3. A motor home is usually owned by a family with _____.

　　A. a baby   B. much money   C. many pets   D. over two kids

( )4. Americans usually use motor homes _____.

　　A. to do some shopping with all the family members

　　B. to travel with all the family members for holidays

　　C. to visit their grandparents at weekends

　　D. to drive their children to school every day

( )5. Motor homes have become popular because _____.

　　A. they can take people to another city when people are free

　　B. some people have much money

　　C. big families can put more things in motor homes

　　D. they can let families have a happier life when they go out for their holidays

第五节　词义搭配:从(B)栏中选出(A)栏单词的正确解释。

　　　　(A)　　　　　　　　　(B)

(　)1. means　　　　　A. confident, expecting the best

(　)2. argue　　　　　B. method or way

(　)3. optimistic　　　　C. dislike, be tired of

(　)4. hate　　　　　D. come in

(　)5. enter　　　　　E. quarrel, express disagreement

第六节 补全对话：根据对话内容，从对话后的选项中选出能填入空白处的最佳选项。

A：Hi, Kate, you look so worried. What's the matter?

B：__1__ I've got a headache, a running nose and a sore throat. You know the A-H1N1 virus(病毒) is so scary. I fear...

A：__2__

B：No, I don't. I took my temperature just now.

A：Don't worry. A fever is the common symptom(症状) of the disease. __3__

B：I hope so.

A：__4__ You can get some advice.

B：That's a good idea. __5__

A：Sure. Let's go.

A. It's a pleasure.
B. Maybe you've just had a cold.
C. Will you please go with me?
D. How long have you been like this?
E. But you'd better go to see a doctor.
F. I'm feeling terrible.
G. Do you have a fever?

第七节 单词拼写。

1. They are _____ (职员) of the big company.

2. He was _____ (吸引) by the scenery on the beach.

3. He felt _____ (沮丧) because of the loss of his wife.

4. They went _____ (上楼) to have a rest.

5. There are several _____ (选择) for you.

第八节 词形变换。

1. Yesterday he had an _____ (argue) with his parents.

2. He _____ (success) finished the job on time.

3. The woman didn't know where her _____ (happy) was.

4. He has an _____ (amaze) attitude to life.

5. The _____ (die) of my dog made me very sad.

第九节 改错：从 A、B、C、D 四个画线处找出一处错误的选项填入括号内，并在横线上写出正确答案。

1. Her parents had the work finish before ten o'clock.
     A   B   C   D

2. Nobody but my teachers know my success.
     A   B   C   D

3. She didn't tell me what should she do.
    A   B   C   D

4. There comes a beautiful girl, doesn't there?
    A   B   C   D

5. He was used to swim in the river when he was young.
         A   B C   D

1. (　　) 应为_____   2. (　　) 应为_____

3. (　　) 应为_____   4. (　　) 应为_____

5. (　　) 应为_____

第十节 作文。

作文题目：Obey the Traffic Rules。

词数要求：80～100 词。

写作要点：1. 随着人口数量的增长和人们生活水平的提高，马路上出现了越来越多的车辆，出现了许多不遵守交通规则的现象。

2. 请结合自己的观点谈谈遵守交通规则的重要性。

3. 参考词汇：pedestrian（行人），cyclist（骑车人），risk（冒险）。

阶段测试题(Unit 1~Unit 2)

第一部分　英语知识运用

（共分三节，满分 40 分）

——★★★——

第一节　语音知识：从 A、B、C、D 四个选项中找出其画线部分与所给单词画线部分读音相同的选项，并在答题卡上将该项涂黑。（共 5 分，每小题 1 分）

(　　)1. s<u>o</u>ciety　　A. c<u>o</u>nversation　　B. p<u>o</u>litely　　C. pr<u>o</u>mise　　D. l<u>o</u>st

(　　)2. c<u>ou</u>gh　　A. acc<u>ou</u>nt　　B. th<u>ou</u>ght　　C. r<u>ou</u>nd　　D. sh<u>ou</u>ld

(　　)3. <u>th</u>us　　A. <u>th</u>rough　　B. <u>th</u>ird　　C. <u>th</u>ough　　D. <u>th</u>irsty

(　　)4. depress<u>ed</u>　　A. miss<u>ed</u>　　B. play<u>ed</u>　　C. tast<u>ed</u>　　D. tir<u>ed</u>

(　　)5. w<u>oo</u>l　　A. f<u>oo</u>d　　B. r<u>oo</u>m　　C. bl<u>oo</u>d　　D. f<u>oo</u>t

第二节　词汇与语法知识：从 A、B、C、D 四个选项中选出可以填入空白处的最佳选项，并在答题卡上将该项涂黑。（共 25 分，每小题 1 分）

(　　)6. The woman is _____ hard working a teacher _____ every student respects her very much.
　　A. so that　　B. so...that　　C. such that　　D. such...that

(　　)7. Don't _____ her _____ outside in the rain.
　　A. leave; waits　　　　　　B. making; at
　　C. leave; waiting　　　　　D. make; to stand

(　　)8. In everyday life, the word "work" has different _____.
　　A. means　　B. meanings　　C. meant　　D. mean

(　　)9. We sometimes do or say something that may _____ others.
　　A. injure　　B. destroy　　C. hurt　　D. wound

15

( )10. Seldom _____ TV programs during the day.

　　A. watch they　　　　　　　B. they are watching

　　C. they watch　　　　　　　D. do they watch

( )11. The house is rather old and it wanted _____.

　　A. be repaired　　B. repairing　　C. to repair　　D. repaired

( )12. No one can avoid _____ by advertisements.

　　A. being influenced　　　　B. influencing

　　C. to be influenced　　　　D. having influence

( )13. I remember we met each other _____ last year.

　　A. some time　　B. sometimes　　C. sometime　　D. some times

( )14. It's really kind _____.

　　A. for you to say so　　　　B. for you saying so

　　C. of you to say so　　　　D. of you saying so

( )15. I have _____ friends except you.

　　A. little　　　　B. a little　　　　C. few　　　　D. a few

( )16. The old woman asked me _____ get there.

　　A. how he can　　B. how can he　　C. how he could　　D. how could he

( )17. Jason is _____ a lecturer, he is a writer, too.

　　A. more than　　B. much than　　C. no more than　　D. as much as

( )18. I will certainly be surprised if he _____ to tell them what he knows.

　　A. dares　　　　B. dared　　　　C. daring　　　　D. dare

( )19. This pair of shoes _____ in fashion now.

　　A. is　　　　　B. are　　　　　C. were　　　　D. was

( )20. Cotton _____ all kinds of cloth.

　　A. is used to waving　　　　B. is used to wave

　　C. used to wave　　　　　　D. use to waving

( )21. Nothing is here, _____?

　　A. are they　　B. aren't they　　C. is it　　D. isn't it

( )22. Only on the top of hill _____ the small hospital.

　　A. We can see　　B. can we see　　C. see we can　　D. see can we

( )23. I find _____ easy _____ English for a Canadian.

　　A. it; learn　　B. that; to learn　　C. it; to learn　　D. that; learning

阶段测试题(Unit 1~Unit 2)

(   )24. At Christmas, children always have _____.
   A. delicious something to eat   B. something to eat delicious
   C. something delicious to eat   D. some delicious thing to eat

(   )25. I insisted that the old man _____ to the People's Hospital.
   A. be sent   B. should send   C. is sent   D. will be sent

(   )26. The young lady _____ a bike is our English teacher.
   A. ride   B. rides   C. rode   D. riding

(   )27. They are looking forward to _____ all over the world.
   A. be traveled   B. traveled   C. traveling   D. travel

(   )28. _____ he tells me the truth, I won't punish him.
   A. As soon as   B. As long as   C. As well as   D. As far as

(   )29. A _____ snake frightened me and I screamed loudly.
   A. 3 meters long B. 3 meter long   C. 3-meter-long D. 3-meters-long

(   )30. The old woman _____ when we got to the hospital.
   A. has died   B. has been died   C. had died   D. died

第三节　完形填空：阅读下面的短文，从所给的每组A、B、C、D四个选项中选择正确的答案，并在答题卡上将该项涂黑。(共10分，每小题1分)

When we communicate with each other 31 gestures or facial expressions, we are engaged in nonverbal communication. It is a way 32 express meaning or feeling without words. For instance, a smile and handshake show welcome. 33 one's hand is to say "Hi" or "Goodbye." When we agree with 34 , we express our opinion by nodding our heads, 35 shaking the head means disagreement. When we cannot 36 a decision, we frown. These gestures are accepted 37 by Chinese and English speakers as having the same meaning.

 38 , people from different cultures may have difficulty in understanding each other's style of nonverbal communication. Thus we see that nonverbal communication is not uniform 39 cultures. However, like language, nonverbal communication carries meaning. Though it is silent, 40 it speaks louder than words.

(   )31. A. through   B. of   C. in   D. with
(   )32. A. at   B. on   C. to   D. in
(   )33. A. Wave   B. Waving   C. Waved   D. To wave

17

(	)34. A. the other	B. another	C. other	D. others
(	)35. A. while	B. so	C. because	D. meanwhile
(	)36. A. have	B. take	C. make	D. made
(	)37. A. either	B. neither	C. all	D. both
(	)38. A. Then	B. Thus	C. However	D. Wherever
(	)39. A. in	B. across	C. cross	D. through
(	)40. A. /	B. but	C. so	D. yet

第二部分　篇章与词汇理解

（共分三节，满分50分）

——★★★——

第一节　阅读理解：阅读下列短文，从每题所给A、B、C、D四个选项中，选出最恰当的答案，并在答题卡上将该项涂黑。（共30分，每小题2分）

A

Several years ago, a television reporter was talking to three of the most important people in America. One was a very rich banker, another owned one of the largest companies in the world, and the third owned many buildings in the center of New York.

The reporter was talking to them about being important.

"How do we know if someone is really important?" the reporter asked the banker.

The banker thought for a few moments and then said, "I think anybody who is invited to the White House to meet the President of the United States is really important."

The reporter then turned to the owner of the very large company. "Do you agree with that?" she asked.

The man shook his head, "No. I think the President invites a lot of people to the White House. You'd only be important if while you were visiting the President, there was a telephone call from the President of another country, and the President of the US said he was too busy to answer it."

The reporter turned to the third man, "Do you think so?"

"No, I don't," he said. "I don't think that makes the visitor important. That makes the President important.

"Then what would make the visitor important?" the reporter and the other two men asked.

"Oh, I think if the visitor to the White House was talking to the President and the phone rang, the President picked up the receiver, listened and then said, ' It's for you.' "

( )41. How many people are there in the passage?
  A. One man and three women.   B. Two men and two women.
  C. Three men and a women.   D. Four men.

( )42. This story happened in _____.
  A. China   B. Australia
  C. the United States   D. England

( )43. The banker thought _____.
  A. the reporter was very important
  B. he himself was very important
  C. the visitor who met the President of America was important
  D. the visitor to the White House was really important

( )44. The owner of the large company thought _____.
  A. the banker was really important
  B. The man owner of many buildings in the center of New York was really important
  C. the reporter was very important
  D. The visitor was important if while he was visiting President, the President would not answer any telephone call

( )45. The owner of many buildings thought _____.
  A. the owner of the very large company was really important
  B. the person who worked in the White House was really important
  C. he was really important because he owned many buildings in the center of New York
  D. the visitor was really important who was talking to the President and the President received a telephone call for the visitor

B

An eight-year-old child heard her parents talking about her little brother. All she

knew was that he was very sick and they had no money. Only a very expensive operation could save him now and there was no one to lend them the money.

When she heard her daddy say to her tearful mother, "Only a miracle can save him now," the little girl went to her bedroom and pulled her money from its hiding place and counted it carefully.

She hurried to a drugstore with the money in her hand.

"And what do you want?" asked the salesman. "It's for my little brother," the girl answered. "He's really sick and I want to buy a miracle." "Pardon?" said the salesman.

"My brother Andrew has something bad growing inside his head and my daddy says only a miracle can save him. So how much does a miracle cost?"

"We don't sell a miracle here, child. I'm sorry." the salesman said with a smile.

"Listen, if it isn't enough, I can try and get some more. Just tell me how much it costs." A well-dressed man heard it and asked, "What kind of a miracle does your brother need?"

"I don't know," she answered with her eyes full of tears. "He's really sick and mum says he needs an operation. But my daddy can't pay for it, so I have brought all my money."

"How much do you have?" asked the man. "1.11 dollars, but I can try and get some more," she answered.

"Well, what luck," smiled the man. "1.11 dollars, the price of a miracle for little brothers."

He took up the girl's hand and said, "Take me to where you live. I want to see your brother and meet your parents. Let's see if I have the kind of miracle you need."

That well-dressed man was Dr Carlton Armstrong, a famous doctor. The operation was successful and it wasn't long before Andrew was home again.

How much did the miracle cost?

(　　)46. What was the trouble in the little girl's family?

　　A. Nothing could save her brother.

　　B. Her brother was seriously ill.

　　C. They have no money.

　　D. both B and C.

(　　)47. In the eyes of the little girl, a miracle might be _____.

  A. some good food   B. some wonderful medicine

  C. something beautiful   D. something interesting

(　　)48. The girl said she could try and get some more, which shows _____.

  A. she hoped not to be refused

  B. she thought money was easy to get

  C. she had still kept some money

  D. there was no need to worry about money

(　　)49. What made the miracle happen?

  A. Nobody can tell.

  B. The girl's money.

  C. The girl's love for her brother.

  D. The medicine from the drugstore.

(　　)50. From the passage we can infer that _____.

  A. The little girl is lovely but not so clever

  B. The doctor didn't ask for any pay

  C. Andrew was in fact not so sick as they had thought

  D. A miracle is sure to happen if you keep on

C

  Last Friday a storm swept through two villages in the New Territories, destroying fourteen homes. Seven others were so badly damaged that their owners had to leave them, and fifteen others had broken windows or broken roofs. One person was killed, several were badly hurt and taken to hospital, and a number of other people received smaller hurt. Altogether over two hundred people were homeless after the storm.

  A farmer, Mr Tan, said that the storm began early in the morning and lasted for over an hour.

  "I was eating with my wife and children," he said, "when we heard a loud noise. A few minutes later our house fell down on top of us. We tried our best to climb out but then I saw that one of my children was missing. I went back inside and found him, safe but very frightened."

  Mrs Woo Mei Fong said that her husband had just left for work when she felt that her house was moving. She ran outside at once with her children.

  "There was no time to take anything," she said, "A few minutes later, the roof came down."

Soldiers helped to take people out of the flooded area and the welfare department brought them food, clothes and shelter.

( )51. What happened on Last Friday?
　　A. There was a big storm.　　B. There was a big flood.
　　C. There was a big earthquake.　　D. There was a big typhoon.

( )52. The underlined word "shelter" in this passage means _____.
　　A. something to drink　　B. something to stay
　　C. something to eat　　D. something to wear

( )53. Where was Mr Tan when the storm first began?
　　A. He was in his office.　　B. He was on the roof.
　　C. He was inside the house.　　D. He was outside the house.

( )54. How many people were homeless in this incident?
　　A. Several.　　B. Fourteen.　　C. Fifteen.　　D. Two hundred.

( )55. Which of the following may be the best title for this passage?
　　A. Clever People.　　B. A Lucky Woman.
　　C. A Terrible Storm.　　D. Good Soldiers.

第二节　词义搭配:从(B)栏中选出(A)栏单词的正确解释,并在答题卡上将该项涂黑。(共10分,每小题1分)

　　　　(A)　　　　　　　　　　　　(B)
( )56. famous　　　　　　A. to ask with force; to ask by ordering
( )57. century　　　　　　B. what something is used for
( )58. finally　　　　　　　C. widely known
( )59. realize　　　　　　　D. go on happening
( )60. polite　　　　　　　E. a period of 100 years
( )61. communicate　　　F. to tell; to give or exchange information
( )62. demand　　　　　　G. at last
( )63. manner　　　　　　H. showing good manners and respect
( )64. continue　　　　　　I. a way of acting or behaving
( )65. purpose　　　　　　J. be fully aware of

第三节 补全对话:根据对话内容,从对话后的选项中选出能填入空白处的最佳选项,并在答题卡上将该项涂黑。(共10分,每小题2分)

J:You look worried this evening,dear. __66__

M:I'm going through the telephone bill. It's over 100 pounds. __67__

J:I don't think we've used the telephone more than usual,have we?

M:But the long-distance calls and telegrams are very high. Who made all these expensive calls to London? I don't remember making them. __68__

J:Oh,they must be Jack's calls. Anne was staying in London with her uncle in October. Jack rang her up nearly every evening.

M:Oh,did he? __69__

L:Jack's only earning 300 pounds a month.

M:What long talks they must have had!

L:Yes,but do remember they are young, __70__ Father sent me a check for Christmas,you remember? I haven't spent it all yet.

M:I wasn't serious,dear. Use your father's money for yourself. I'm sure there are lots of things you like.

A. Do you know anyone in London?
B. What's the trouble?
C. Well,he can pay for the calls,then
D. I will pay for Jack's calls to Ann.
E. Last month it was under 70 pounds.

第三部分 语言技能运用

(共分四节,满分30分)

——★★★——

第一节 单词拼写:根据下列句子及所给汉语注释,在答题卡上相应题号后的横线上写出该单词。(共5分,每小题1分)

71. We can talk with the help of _____ (手势),eye contact and facial expressions.

72. I don't think the job is _____ (适合) for you.

73. A pretty dog _____ (吸引) the gentleman and he wants to own it.

74. The young man works hard, and he is always _____ (精力充沛的).

75. How many people were _____ (伤害) in this accident?

第二节　词形变换：用括号内单词的适当形式填空，将正确答案写在答题卡上相应题号后的横线上。(共 5 分，每小题 1 分)

76. From his _____ (express), we know the truth.

77. The old man in that big battle tried to make his story _____ (live).

78. The old man states his meaning _____ (succeed).

79. It is difficult for him to make a _____ (decide) at once.

80. Why was the woman _____ (not understand) by his husband?

第三节　改错：从 A、B、C、D 四个画线处找出一处错误的选项填入答题卡上相应题号后的括号内，并在横线上写出正确答案。(共 10 分，每小题 2 分)

( )81. Either <u>his parents</u> or <u>his wife</u> <u>know</u> where he <u>has gone</u>.
　　　　　　A　　　　　　B　　　　C　　　　　D

( )82. <u>One third</u> <u>of</u> oil <u>are</u> <u>wasted</u> by man.
　　　　A　　　B　　　C　　D

( )83. <u>It is no good</u> <u>to buy</u> so many clothes <u>in</u> her <u>ninth</u> month.
　　　　A　　　　　　B　　　　　　　　C　　　D

( )84. <u>The young man</u> <u>left</u> his room, <u>took</u> <u>nothing</u>.
　　　　A　　　　　B　　　　　　C　　D

( )85. They didn't tell her <u>what</u> <u>would</u> <u>she</u> <u>do</u> next step.
　　　　　　　　　　　A　　　B　　C　　D

81. (　　) 应为 _____　　　82. (　　) 应为 _____
83. (　　) 应为 _____　　　84. (　　) 应为 _____
85. (　　) 应为 _____

第四节　书面表达。(共 10 分)

作文题目：How to Be Successful。

词数要求：80～100 词。

写作要点：1. 你认为怎样才算成功？
　　　　　2. 通过哪些努力才能成功？

Unit 3 Fashion

单元基础知识闯关小测验

I. 汉译英。

1. 踏入_____ 2. 穿上_____ 3. 躺下_____
4. 穿坏_____ 5. 一段历史_____ 6. 总而言之_____
7. 把……制成_____   8. 控制_____

II. 词形变换。

1. comfortable _____ (反义词)   2. French _____ (国名)
3. gradual _____ (副词)   4. various _____ (动词)
5. strength _____ (动词)   6. fashion _____ (形容词)

III. 用括号内所给词的适当形式填空。

1. The story was so _____ (interest) that all of the pupils were _____ (interest) in it.

2. There were some strangers _____ (sit) at the back of the classroom.

3. The building _____ (build) now is our new dormitory.

4. The criminal came in _____ (follow) by two policemen.

5. The speaker raised his voice to make himself _____ (hear).

6. _____ (hear) the exciting news, the children jumped with joy.

单元综合练习

★★★

第一节 语音知识：从 A、B、C、D 四个选项中找出其画线部分与所给单词画线部分读音相同的选项。

( )1. pattern   A. fat   B. relate   C. salad   D. pace

( )2. serve   A. watcher   B. prefer   C. miner   D. order

( )3. licence   A. seldom   B. step   C. strength   D. parent

( )4. vary   A. grammar   B. dark   C. ward   D. various

( )5. instantly   A. liquor   B. diet   C. wine   D. line

第二节 词汇与语法知识：从 A、B、C、D 四个选项中选出可以填入空白处的最佳选项。

( )1. The boy stepped _____ the boat and went away with his friends.
    A. in   B. into   C. out   D. off

( )2. These American visitors were all _____ in Chinese traditional clothes.
    A. dressed   B. wearing   C. put on   D. have on

( )3. The miners _____ their normal pants very easily.
    A. wears out   B. run out   C. ran out   D. wore out

( )4. The boss told the workers that they had to make the work _____ before 8 o'clock.
    A. finish   B. finishing   C. to finish   D. finished

( )5. They didn't intend _____ the decision, but they had to.
    A. make   B. making   C. to make   D. made

( )6. We all know that butter is made _____ milk.
    A. of   B. out of   C. from   D. up of

( )7. They haven't decided _____ during the coming winter holiday.
    A. when to go   B. where to go   C. why to do   D. what to go

( )8. It was _____ his father came back that he had dinner.
    A. not until   B. until   C. till   D. no until

( )9. _____ the composition, he left school and went home.
    A. Finish   B. Finished
    C. Having finished   D. finishing

( )10. We must _____ some notice of what the chairman said.
A. take B. make C. get D. pay

( )11. —Let's go shopping tomorrow, shall we?
—_____
A. Yes, let's go. B. It is my pleasure.
C. It doesn't matter. D. I agree with you.

( )12. In the 1960's, the scientist went back to his motherland. What is the meaning of the underlined phrase?
A. 在 1960 年 B. 在 20 世纪 50 年代
C. 在 19 世纪 60 年代 D. 在 20 世纪 60 年代

( )13. Tom _____ buttons for his grandpa every day.
A. does on B. does up C. runs of D. uses up

( )14. Mr Harper doesn't know what type of dress is _____ for his wife.
A. suit B. suits C. suitable D. suitably

( )15. On weekends, the twins prefer _____ at home reading rather than _____ with their mother.
A. to stay... go shopping B. stay... going shopping
C. staying... going home D. to stay... to go shopping

( )16. The child is considered _____ by all his friends.
A. honesty B. honest C. honestly D. honester

( )17. Mary was very depressed for _____ to the party.
A. being not invited B. not being invited
C. having not being invited D. not having been invited

( )18. _____ a month ago, the furniture is expected to arrive at any time now.
A. Ordered B. Ordering C. Being ordered D. To order

( )19. Because of the young racing through daytime meals, _____ is becoming more and more popular.
A. dinnering out B. dining out C. dinner out D. dine out

( )20. —What is his sister like?
—_____
A. She is pretty. B. She is tall.
C. She likes playing the piano. D. She is a very nice person.

第三节 完形填空:阅读下面的短文,从所给的 A、B、C、D 四个选项中选出最佳的答案。

Not long ago, Kim and Tucci from Perth Australia, welcomed their __1__ healthy babies at a time—a son and four daughters. Suddenly they seemed to become the __2__ but busiest parents in the world.

Recently Tucci has shared some photos of her lovely babies. One of __3__ shows that the 26-year-old mom is __4__ and holding her five tiny babies in her arms.

There will be more challenges the parents have to face in the future. "Sometimes I lock myself in the bathroom and cry on the floor," Tucci said on the TV program 60 Minutes. "We have to change 350 dirty diapers(尿布) __5__ and feed each baby eight times a day. Although the work may be terrible, it's worth __6__. No one thought I could do it, but I did. I'm actually proud of __7__ now."

All her five babies have surprised a lot of people. When they were born, each __8__ more than one kilo and seemed very __9__. Now more and more people are trying to help and support the family. We expect all the babies can grow up __10__ and have a good future.

( )1. A. four   B. three   C. five   D. one
( )2. A. happiest   B. happy   C. happier   D. happily
( )3. A. which   B. whom   C. them   D. they
( )4. A. lying   B. lay   C. lie   D. lied
( )5. A. a day   B. a month   C. an hour   D. a week
( )6. A. do   B. did   C. doing   D. does
( )7. A. me   B. myself   C. we   D. our
( )8. A. weigh   B. weight   C. weighed   D. weighing
( )9. A. healthy   B. health   C. healthily   D. unhealthy
( )10. A. healthy   B. health   C. healthily   D. unhealthy

第四节 阅读理解:阅读下列短文,从每题所给 A、B、C、D 四个选项中,选出最恰当的答案。

Parents Are Important in Our Life

Mom and Dad are two of the most important people in your life. All through your lifetime, they may influence(影响) you more than anyone else whom you will meet. So if your mom loves to read, you just might grow up carrying a book wherever you go, just as she does. But parents do a lot more than just pass on their hobbies. Moms and Dads need to care for their kids the minute their kids are born. Most parents will do this as long as they live.

Here are some ways you can get along well and build a strong relationship with your parents.

Spend time together. Instead of playing computer games or watching TV, ask your mom and dad to play with you. Go outside together, or do some reading.

Be kind. Little things might mean a lot to your mom or dad. You can brighten (使生辉)a parent's day with a hug or a joke. It's also lovely when a kid cleans up his or her room without being asked. And if you try not to fight with your brothers or sisters, your parents will also be happy!

Try your best at whatever you do. You don't have to be perfect, but when you do your best, you make your parents proud. It makes them happy to see how you're turning into a great kid, because you are their most love in the world.

(　　)1. Who may influence you more than anyone else according to the passage?

　　A. Teachers.　　　　　　B. Parents.

　　C. The people you meet.　　D. Friends.

(　　)2. Which of the following can't help you stay close with your parents?

　　A. Spending time together.

　　B. Being kind.

　　C. Watching TV.

　　D. Doing your best at whatever you do.

(　　)3. Your parents will be unhappy if you _____.

　　A. clean up his or her room without being asked

　　B. play computer games for too much time

　　C. try your best to do something

　　D. give them a hug

(　　)4. What does the underlined part in the passage mean? It means _____.

　　A. they make you become a good kid

　　B. they work hard

　　C. they care for your progress

D. they do well in their office work

(   )5. If a mother likes reading, her kids will _____.

    A. like playing computers   B. also like reading

    C. like watching TV   D. hate reading

第五节 词义搭配:从(B)栏中选出(A)栏单词的正确解释。

        (A)   (B)

(   )1. jeans   A. rarely, not often

(   )2. pattern   B. trousers dressed in working

(   )3. remove   C. make, produce

(   )4. seldom   D. take to another place

(   )5. manufacture   E. somebody or something serving as a model

第六节 补全对话:根据对话内容,从对话后的选项中选出能填入空白处的最佳选项。

M: Good morning.   1

W: Yes, please. Could you introduce a nice place to visit during the summer vacation?

M: OK. Dalian is a nice place to visit. It's the right time to go there.   2

W: Sounds good.   3

M: You can go there by plane.

W: Shall I visit some places of interest by car in Dalian?

M: Sure. Our sightseeing bus will take you around the city.

W: Really perfect.   4

M: 280 yuan per person. It includes train tickets, park tickets, hotel and meals.

W: Well. It's nice.   5

```
A. How much does it cost?
B. I'd like to book the tour for three.
C. The weather is neither hot nor cold.
D. How can I get there?
E. What can I do for you, madam?
```

Unit 3 Fashion

第七节　单词拼写。

1. The type of cloth is only m＿＿＿＿＿（生产）in the south France.
2. It takes both rain and sunlight to create a ＿＿＿＿＿（彩虹）.
3. The food in this restaurant is ＿＿＿＿＿（定价）high.
4. These tickets for the park are ＿＿＿＿＿（可用的）for only one month.
5. Mother bought Peter some ＿＿＿＿＿（合适的）clothes for winter.

第八节　词形变换。

1. The students entered the lecture hall ＿＿＿＿＿（follow） their professor.
2. They will visit the City Library ＿＿＿＿＿（build） last year.
3. The leaders of the two countries are willing to ＿＿＿＿＿（strong）the relationship between them.
4. Lying on so hard a bed, the old man felt very ＿＿＿＿＿（comfort）.
5. Young girls like wearing ＿＿＿＿＿（fashion） dresses when attending a dinner.

第九节　改错：从 A、B、C、D 四个画线处找出一处错误的选项填入括号内，并在横线上写出正确答案。

1. Have watered the vegetables, they had a break.
   　A　　　　　　B　　　　　C　　　D
2. He told me that Rose had had her hair dying into red.
   　　A　　　　　　B　　C　　　　　　D
3. Food is close related to one's life and health.
   　　　　A　　B　　　　C　　　　D
4. Now, blue jeans having a rainbow of colors and styles is in fashion.
   　　　　　　　A　　　　B　　　　　　　　　　C　　D
5. The rivets used strengthen the jeans were removed in the crotch.
   　　　　　A　　　B　　　　　　　C　　　　　D

1.（　）应为＿＿＿＿＿　　　　2.（　）应为＿＿＿＿＿
3.（　）应为＿＿＿＿＿　　　　4.（　）应为＿＿＿＿＿
5.（　）应为＿＿＿＿＿

第十节　作文。

作文题目：Advertisements。

词数要求：80～100 词。

写作要点：1. 人们对广告有不同的看法。一些人认为广告能拓宽人们对商品的选择，另外一些人认为广告很令人讨厌，消费者经常被虚假广告欺骗。

　　　　　2. 谈谈你的观点。

Unit 4 Colors and Mood

单元基础知识闯关小测验

I. 汉译英。

1. 因……被罚款_____   2. 在……的控制下_____

3. 从……移动到…… _____   4. 指的是, 提及_____

5. 情绪低落_____   6. 爱信不信_____

7. 警告某人某事_____   8. 火冒三丈_____

II. 词形变换。

1. pleasant _____（反义词）   2. associate _____（名词）

3. policeman _____（复数形式）   4. connection _____（动词）

5. effect _____（动词）   6. choose _____（形容词）

III. 选择正确答案。

(   ) 1. Only then _____ that he had done something wrong.
   A. he realize   B. realized he   C. did he realize   D. do they realize

(   ) 2. Never _____ since they left the factory last year.
   A. they have met   B. have they met
   C. had they met   D. they had met

(   ) 3. —He likes playing basketball very much.
   —_____
   A. So does he.   B. So he does.   C. Nor does he.   D. Nor he does.

(   )4. _____, I would accept the invitation.

    A. I were you   B. I you were   C. If were I you   D. Were I you

(   )5. Out _____ when the bell rang.

    A. rush the children   B. rush they

    C. rushed the children   D. rushed they

(   )6. There _____ a trainer and some players on the playground.

    A. are   B. have   C. be   D. is

单元综合练习

★★★

第一节　语音知识：从 A、B、C、D 四个选项中找出其画线部分与所给单词画线部分读音相同的选项。

(   )1. shape   A. rate   B. associate   C. affect   D. avoid

(   )2. carpet   A. warn   B. particular   C. share   D. regard

(   )3. choosy   A. foot   B. classroom   C. wool   D. mood

(   )4. accept   A. factor   B. announce   C. affect   D. calm

(   )5. achieve   A. believe   B. diet   C. friend   D. science

第二节　词汇与语法知识：从 A、B、C、D 四个选项中选出可以填入空白处的最佳选项。

(   )1. Hearing the good news, he seemed so _____ that he could say a word.

    A. excited   B. excite   C. exciting   D. excitedly

(   )2. Will you answer the phone? It _____ be your brother.

    A. may   B. must   C. can   D. need

(   )3. Which color do you _____, red or blue?

    A. preferring   B. preferred   C. like best   D. prefer

(   )4. Computers have a great effect _____ people's life.

    A. in   B. on   C. into   D. out

(   )5. _____ does he write well, _____ he also speaks well.

    A. Not...but   B. Not only...but also

    C. Not only...but   D. Never...but

(   )6. It is reported that pet animals _____ make people happy.

A. intend to   B. lead to   C. tend to   D. result of

(   )7. His parents seemed _____ with her marks in the examination.

A. pleasing   B. pleased   C. pleasant   D. to please

(   )8. This apple is bigger than _____ on the plate.

A. any other one   B. all the apples   C. other ones   D. anything other

(   )9. She spent a lot of money _____ clothes and dressing.

A. in   B. into   C. on   D. out

(   )10. Her parents won't allow her _____ out late.

A. to stay   B. staying   C. stayed   D. stay

(   )11. —My brother never read books in bed.

—_____.

A. So does he   B. So he does

C. Nor does my sister   D. Nor may sister does

(   )12. Most people like spring, because it _____ life.

A. is associated to   B. associate with

C. associate to   D. is associated with

(   )13. The children _____ the danger of the bridge.

A. warned of   B. are warned of

C. warn for   D. are warned for

(   )14. —Good morning! Can you lend me a hand?

—_____.

A. Yes, please   B. No, thanks   C. Certainly   D. Thank you

(   )15. When people are in a good mood, they are _____.

A. in high spirits   B. in high spirit   C. in a high spirit   D. in highly spirits

(   )16. When the teacher praised someone in class, he _____ you.

A. refer to   B. referred to   C. referring to   D. is referred to

(   )17. Books are of great _____ in people's daily life.

A. valuable   B. valuablly   C. valuably   D. value

(   )18. In the stock market, blue-chip is a _____ and safe share.

A. promising   B. promise   C. promised   D. promises

(   )19. The old photos hanging on the wall _____ the old man _____ his childhood.

A. reminds... in B. reminded... in
C. reminded... of D. remind... in

( )20. Leifeng _____ a hero, whom we should learn from.

A. is regard as B. was regarded as
C. was regarded so D. is regarded as

第三节 完形填空：阅读下面的短文，从所给的 A、B、C、D 四个选项中选出最佳的答案。

A Taxi Driver

My friend is a __1__ driver. He has been a taxi driver for ten years. It's a nice __2__ most of the time. He can meet a lot of people. He always works __3__ because there is too much traffic during the day. He usually goes home between two o'clock in the morning. There are some very strange things, __4__ often happen at night. One day my friend was taking a woman back home from a party at three o'clock in the morning. She had her little dog __5__ her. When they got to her house, she found she had lost her __6__. So my friend waited in the car with the dog while she climbed in through the __7__. My friend waited and waited. After half an hour of honking he decided to find out __8__ was going on. He tied the dog to a tree and started to climb in through the window. At that moment some __9__ came. They thought my friend was a thief. Luckily, the woman came downstairs. She __10__ have gone to sleep and forgotten about my friend and the dog.

( )1. A. bus B. taxi C. train D. bike
( )2. A. work B. works C. jobs D. job
( )3. A. at night B. in the day
    C. in the afternoon D. in the morning
( )4. A. which B. that C. who D. whom
( )5. A. in B. out of C. with D. on
( )6. A. bag B. key C. money D. phone
( )7. A. window B. door C. gate D. step
( )8. A. that B. which C. whom D. what
( )9. A. thieves B. workers C. policemen D. policeman
( )10. A. may B. must C. can D. might

第四节　阅读理解：阅读下列短文，从每题所给 A、B、C、D 四个选项中，选出最恰当的答案。

The Old Farmer

Once upon a time, there was an old farmer who lived on his farm which was far away from the city. He had never been to the city and spent almost all his life on his farm in the countryside. Often hearing that the city was amazing and interesting, one day, he decided to visit the big city.

When he got there, everything was new and strange to him, because this was the first time he had traveled to the city. Wandering in the street, he wondered why there were so many people and why they looked so young and beautiful.

At last, he went into a large hotel and saw an elevator. While he was watching, an old lady got into the elevator and closed the door. Then, the elevator run up quickly and after a while, it came back again. The door opened and a very pretty young girl came out. The old farmer was amazed and satisfied. "What an incredible little room it is!" he said to himself happily, "How wonderful! It is no wonder that the citizens look so pretty and young. The room can change an old woman into a young pretty girl. The next time I come here, I'm going to bring my wife along."

(　　) 1. The old farmer lived _____.

　　A. on the farm　　　　　　　B. in the city

　　C. near the city　　　　　　D. in a large tall building

(　　) 2. Why did the old farmer decide to go to the city one day?

　　A. He hated living in the country.　　B. He heard the city was fun.

　　C. He decided to visit a factory.　　　D. He wanted to visit a hotel.

(　　) 3. Did the old farmer like the city?

　　A. No, he didn't.　　　　　　B. Yes, he did.

　　C. We don't know.　　　　　D. It depends on.

(　　) 4. When the old farmer was in the large tall building, he found _____ come out of the lift.

　　A. a young girl　　B. an old man　　C. his wife　　D. an old woman

(　　) 5. From the passage, we can guess the old farmer _____.

　　A. knew the lift well　　　　　B. didn't like the lift

　　C. wanted to buy a lift　　　　D. didn't know anything about the lift

Unit 4 Colours and Mood

第五节 词义搭配:从(B)栏中选出(A)栏单词的正确解释。

　　　　(A)　　　　　　　　　(B)

( )1. shape　　　　A. to give notice of possible danger

( )2. guest　　　　B. keep away from; escape

( )3. warn　　　　 C. a person at another person's house

( )4. avoid　　　　D. concern; attention; respect

( )5. regard　　　 E. outer form

第六节 补全对话:根据对话内容,从对话后的选项中选出能填入空白处的最佳选项。

Peter: What can we do this weekend, Paul? I don't want to do my homework all day.

Paul: I know, Peter. 1

Peter: No, we can't. My dad has to work at home.

Paul: How about a film? Tom's going to see *Paddington Bear* at the cinema. We can go with him.

Peter: 2

Paul: Maybe we can do some shopping then. There's a new cartoon shop opening on Saturday.

Peter: 3

Paul: On the corner of First Street.

Peter: 4

Paul: Well, shall we go by bike? My little brother is going to visit the museum. We can take him there by bike, and then we can go shopping together.

Peter: 5

```
A. Where is the shop?
B. How do we get there?
C. No, I don't want to see a film.
D. That's a great idea.
E. Let's have a party at your house.
```

第七节　单词拼写。

1. A traffic ticket can leave people unpleasant _____ (印象).

2. Standing in front of so many people, the girl felt very _____ (紧张的).

3. According to some _____ (科学的) research, children prefer red and orange.

4. An _____ (联想) is the mental connection between two things or ideas.

5. On his way home, the boy was beaten black and blue, so his body was covered with _____ (伤痕).

第八节　词形变换。

1. Do you think there is some _____ (connect) between one's intelligence and the food one eats?

2. Knowledge of colors preference is of important _____ (apply) in life.

3. Soft music _____ (easy) one's emotion and slows one's heart rate.

4. _____ (calm) colors, like blue and green, tend to make people stay longer in the restaurant.

5. _____ (decorate) with colorful balloons, the room is very beautiful.

第九节　改错：从 A、B、C、D 四个画线处找出一处错误的选项填入括号内, 并在横线上写出正确答案。

1. The reason that he was late was that the traffic was heavy.
　　　　　　 A 　　 B 　　　　 C 　 D

2. As a child, he is in the control of his parents.
　　 A 　　　　 B C 　　　　　　 D

3. I suggest to go for an outing next Sunday.
　　　 A 　 B 　　 C 　 D

4. Failed in the exam, he was afraid to go back home.
　 A 　　　　　　　　 B 　 C 　 D

5. If someone is in low spirits, we say he is in bad mood.
　　　　　　 A 　　 B 　　　　　　 C D

1. (　) 应为_____　　　2. (　) 应为_____

3. (　) 应为_____　　　4. (　) 应为_____

5. (　) 应为_____

第十节　作文。

作文题目：My Favourite Color。

词数要求：80～100 词。

写作要点：1. 写出你最喜欢的颜色。

　　　　　2. 你为什么喜欢这种颜色。

阶段测试题(Unit 3~Unit 4)

第一部分 英语知识运用

（共分三节,满分 40 分）

★★★

第一节 语音知识:从 A、B、C、D 四个选项中找出其画线部分与所给单词画线部分读音相同的选项,并在答题卡上将该项涂黑。(共 5 分,每小题 1 分)

( )1. f<u>i</u>ne   A. r<u>i</u>bbon   B. sh<u>i</u>ft   C. l<u>i</u>quor   D. t<u>i</u>e

( )2. sugge<u>sti</u>on   A. cau<u>ti</u>on   B. rela<u>ti</u>on   C. que<u>sti</u>on   D. connec<u>ti</u>on

( )3. reg<u>ar</u>d   A. c<u>ar</u>pet   B. w<u>ar</u>n   C. sh<u>ar</u>e   D. w<u>ar</u>d

( )4. int<u>e</u>nd   A. v<u>e</u>hicle   B. st<u>e</u>p   C. b<u>e</u>lieve   D. r<u>e</u>fer

( )5. c<u>a</u>lm   A. tot<u>a</u>lly   B. s<u>a</u>lt   C. h<u>a</u>lf   D. soci<u>a</u>l

第二节 词汇与语法知识：从 A、B、C、D 四个选项中选出可以填入空白处的最佳选项,并在答题卡上将该项涂黑。(共 25 分,每小题 1 分)

( )6. He seemed so _____ that he couldn't say a word.
    A. excited   B. excite   C. exciting   D. to excite

( )7. Will you answer the phone, Ada? It _____ be your brother.
    A. mustn't   B. can   C. may   D. need

( )8. Which colors do you _____, the warm colors or the cool colors?
    a. like   B. prefer   C. enjoy   D. interest

( )9. Computers have a great effect _____ people's life.
    A. in   B. at   C. off   D. on

( )10. —It is said that the old woman is a famous scientist.
    —_____.

  A. So she is   B. So she does   C. So is she   D. So does she

( )11. _____ does he speak well, _____ he also writes well.

  A. Neither...nor   B. Not only...but also

  C. Not only...but   D. Either...or

( )12. It's reported that pet owners tend _____ happier than those who don't keep pets.

  A. getting   B. get   C. got   D. to get

( )13. —Please hurry up, or we'll be late.

  —_____.

  A. I come.   B. I would come.   C. I'm coming.   D. I will come.

( )14. Winter is coming and the weather is _____ colder and colder.

  A. became   B. become   C. becoming   D. becomes

( )15. I have never heard someone who sings _____ than she.

  A. best   B. well   C. good   D. better

( )16. Buying books often _____ him about half of his salary.

  A. takes   B. costs   C. spends   D. pays

( )17. The lady was not permitted _____ the room.

  A. to enter   B. entering   C. enter   D. entered

( )18. A friend is someone _____ you are willing to lend a helping hand.

  A. whom   B. who   C. to whom   D. to who

( )19. _____! The University Entrance Exam is coming.

  A. How flies time   B. How time flies

  C. What flies time   D. What time flies

( )20. —What do you _____ my new car?

  —Oh, it is very cool.

  A. think with   B. think over   C. think at   D. think about

( )21. The girls felt so _____ at the _____ news.

  A. surprised...surprised   B. surprised...surprising

  C. surprising...surprised   D. surprising...surprising

( )22. So hard _____ that he succeeded in the end.

  A. does work he   B. does he work

  C. did he work   D. he did work

( )23. Do you know why the girl is _____?
   A. in a bad mood   B. in bad mood
   C. in a low spirit   D. in low spirit

( )24. To protect their kingdom, the emperor ordered to have the walls _____.
   A. linking   B. link   C. to link   D. linked

( )25. She was made _____ another two hours after work every day.
   A. work   B. working   C. to work   D. worked

( )26. You have _____ your buttons in the wrong way.
   A. do up   B. done up   C. tie up   D. done on

( )27. The theory of five elements is turned to be _____.
   A. reasonable   B. reason   C. reasonably   D. unreasonably

( )28. _____ hard before, you would have passed the exam.
   A. If had you studied   B. Had you studied
   C. If you studied   D. Has you studied

( )29. When I entered the room, I found a baby _____ on the ground.
   A. lied   B. laying   C. lying   D. lain

( )30. The thief came into the house without _____.
   A. seeing   B. being seen   C. having seen   D. seen

第三节　完形填空: 阅读下面的短文,从所给的每组 A、B、C、D 四个选项中选择正确的答案,并在答题卡上将该项涂黑。(共 10 分,每小题 1 分)

　　I worked for a short time as a cashier at a ＿＿31＿＿ a few months ago. I also helped to clean up the tables when it was very busy. One night, just before ＿＿32＿＿, I found a large black wallet on the floor near one of the tables. I guessed I should check it to find out ＿＿33＿＿ was the owner, but I was very busy at the time. And I imagined that ＿＿34＿＿ there was something valuable in the wallet, the owner would be back. Surely enough, an hour later a man came in and asked if anyone had found a ＿＿35＿＿. After he described it exactly, I gave him the wallet. He expressed his ＿＿36＿＿ when I handed it to him. He asked me if I had opened it, and I told him "no." At once he opened it and showed that it had nearly ＄800 in cash. He took out a twenty-dollar bill and handed it to me and I was amazed at this. "A reward for your ＿＿37＿＿." he said and walked away.

  38   about it later, I thought if I had no way to find the owner and no one returned to get it, I might keep it. But it also came   39   my mind that I actually saved someone's Christmas plans by returning the wallet. The good feeling was worth more than   40   money could buy.

(　)31. A. hotel　　　B. bank　　　　C. restaurant　　D. school
(　)32. A. Christmas　　　　　　　　B. festival
　　　　C. Thanksgiving Day　　　　D. weekend
(　)33. A. what　　　B. who　　　　C. whom　　　　D. that
(　)34. A. whether　B. weather　　C. where　　　　D. if
(　)35. A. wallet　　B. money　　　C. bag　　　　　D. handbag
(　)36. A. thank　　B. thanks　　　C. thank you　　D. thanking
(　)37. A. honest　 B. honestly　　C. honester　　　D. honesty
(　)38. A. Think　　B. Thinking　　C. Thought　　　D. Thinks
(　)39. A. to　　　　B. into　　　　C. at　　　　　　D. in
(　)40. A. something B. nothing　　C. everything　　D. anything

第二部分　篇章与词汇理解

（共分三节，满分50分）

―――★★★―――

第一节　阅读理解：阅读下列短文，从每题所给A、B、C、D四个选项中，选出最恰当的答案，并在答题卡上将该项涂黑。（共30分，每小题2分）

A

Once my father and I went to see a circus. A family was standing in front of us waiting for tickets. The family had eight children. Their clothes were not expensive but they were clean. They were talking about the clowns and elephants excitedly.

"I want ten tickets, eight for children and two for adults." said the father to the ticket lady. The ticket lady told him the price.

When he heard that, the man couldn't believe his ears. He asked again, "How much?"

The ticket lady spoke again. The father looked sad. Clearly, he didn't have enough money. My dad took a $20 bill and dropped it on the ground. Then he picked up the bill, and said to the man, "Sir, this fell out of your pocket."

The man knew what was going on. He looked into my dad's eyes and took the bill. "Thank you, thank you sir. This really means a lot to me and my family."

We didn't go to the circus that night, but we didn't feel sorry for it at all.

(　　)41. How many people were there in the man's family?

  A. 8.   B. 2.   C. 6.   D. 10.

(　　)42. Did the children see the circus in the end?

  A. No, they didn't.   B. Yes, they did.

  C. No, they did.   D. We don't know.

(　　)43. Who helped the big family?

  A. The police.   B. The boss of the circus.

  C. My father.   D. The ticket lady.

(　　)44. Why didn't the writer see the circus that night?

  A. They had no money.

  B. They gave the money to the family.

  C. They didn't want to see it.

  D. They lost the money.

(　　)45. What did the passage want to tell us?

  A. Being kind to others is important.

  B. The writer's father was clever.

  C. Both of them were glad to help others.

  D. The big family were very happy.

B

I stood in the doorway, watching my older brother carefully putting clothes into his bag. I coughed uneasily. Finally realizing that I was there, Andy turned towards me with a sad smile.

"I'm leaving tomorrow," he said.

"I know." My voice was almost a whisper. I was angry at myself for being so weak, but I wasn't about to cry.

"My flight is early tomorrow, so there is still enough time to come to the airport," he said. Seeing the sad look on my face, he quickly added, "I promise I won't leave without saying goodbye."

I tried to say something, but I didn't. It's always better to keep quiet if you're about to cry. "You promised you wouldn't cry." he said to me, thinking that I was close to tears.

I remembered the day he taught me how to ride a bike. At first, I thought he was always right behind me, holding the seat to keep me from falling. I was happy with this, but he knew he couldn't hold me up all my life. He told me that one day he would have to let me go.

His coughing stopped my thinking. What was left to say? How could I say goodbye to the person who taught me everything?

The next morning I woke up, looked at my alarm clock, and realized he had left hours ago. We never even said goodbye.

Goodbye, Andy! Although he may have been many miles away, I knew he heard me, even if it was only an answer in his heart.

( )46. Why was the writer sad?

 A. Because he was going to leave.

 B. Because Andy was going to leave.

 C. Because his mother was going to leaving.

 D. Because he didn't want to leave.

( )47. Why didn't the writer say Goodbye to his brother?

 A. Because he didn't want him to go.

 B. Because his brother's flight was so early.

 C. Because he saw his brother off at the airport.

 D. Because he was overslept.

( )48. What did Andy teach the writer to do according to the passage?

 A. To ride a bike.   B. To do everything.

 C. To study.   D. To say Goodbye.

( )49. Who was Andy?

 A. A student.   B. An adult.

 C. We don't know.   D. The writer's brother.

( )50. What is the best title of the passage?

 A. My Brother.   B. Brother Taught Me to Ride.

 C. Goodbye, brother!   D. Brother and I.

C

My parents took me to France when I was little. I lived there for six years. When I came back, my French was very good. "Can I do something useful with my French?" I asked myself.

Then one day last spring, I got a good opportunity. Everyone was afraid of going out because of an epidemic, so I stayed at home with nothing to do. My father brought me a French book. "Why don't you translate it into Chinese? It will be better than playing computer games all day."

I promised to do 2,000 words each day. But soon I found it was hard to keep the promise. One day in May, the weather was beautiful. But I couldn't go out. Those 2,000 words were still waiting for me. After translating only three pages, I already lost interest in the book.

I looked at it for a long time. But I couldn't make myself turn the pages. How I wished I could go outside and play football with my friends! I counted the words again and again. I just wanted to give up.

I felt as if two people were fighting in my mind. One said, "Don't give up! Keep working hard, and you'll do well!" But then the other one said, "Go and play! It will be more fun than translating. Do your work tomorrow."

I stood up and went to turn off the computer. But then I remembered what my parents had told me: "Whatever you do, don't stop halfway." So I sat down and went on with it.

(   )51. What foreign language did the writer do well in?

  A. Chinese.   B. English.   C. French.   D. France.

(   )52. What did his father advise him to do?

  A. To translate a book into Chinese.

  B. To translate a book into English.

  C. To translate a book into French.

  D. To play more games.

(   )53. Did the writer once want to give up?

  A. No, he didn't.   B. Yes, he did.

  C. No, he did.   D. Yes, he didn't.

(   )54. Why did he keep on translating the book?

A. He wants to play football with his friends.

B. He didn't want to turn the pages.

C. His father's words made him keep his promise.

D. He wants to stay at home.

(   )55. What is the main idea of the passage?

A. Translating a book is good.

B. Never give up, then you will succeed.

C. Parents are always right.

D. Don't make a promise easily.

第二节　词义搭配:从(B)栏中选出(A)栏单词的正确解释,并在答题卡上将该项涂黑。(共10分,每小题1分)

(A)	(B)
(　)56. available	A. material made by weaving (cotton,silk,wool,etc.)
(　)57. strengthen	B. able to be used
(　)58. allow	C. being present in a place
(　)59. pardon	D. of or in the mind
(　)60. cloth	E. entirely different; contrary
(　)61. mental	F. make or become stronger
(　)62. opposite	G. forgive, not angry
(　)63. fashion	H. permit, let somebody do something
(　)64. presence	I. make somebody think of something; arouse
(　)65. remind	J. something that is popular at a certain time

第三节　补全对话:根据对话内容,从对话后的选项中选出能填入空白处的最佳选项,并在答题卡上将该项涂黑。(共10分,每小题2分)

King: ＿66＿ You look very tired today.

Linda: It's my neighbor's dog. He kept barking and barking. I couldn't sleep last
　　　　night.

King: That's too bad. ＿67＿

Linda: I'm afraid not. He looks rough. None of his neighbors would like to talk to
　　　　him.

King: Sounds bad! Noise is a real problem in our life today.

Linda: __68__ Another of my neighbors plays his TV set loudly late into the night, and still another neighbor plays his C's loudly, too.

King: I feel sorry for you. My neighborhood is quiet, but where I work, it's always noisy. It seems they are advertising all the time.

Linda: Well, I guess either we move to the countryside, or we're used to all the noise.

King: __69__

Linda: I said, we'll have to get used to this city noise.

King: Speak louder! __70__

    A. Have you talked to your neighbor about the problem?
    B. I can't hear you. My motorbike is too loud!
    C. I fully agree with you.
    D. What?
    E. What's the matter with you, Linda?

第三部分　语言技能运用

（共分四节，满分30分）

——★★★——

第一节　单词拼写：根据下列句子及所给汉语注释，在答题卡上相应题号后的横线上写出该单词。（共5分，每小题1分）

71. People who like warm colors must be _____（乐观的）.

72. Most fast-food _____（饭店）avoid cool colors.

73. Their _____（标准的）food is reasonably priced and instantly available.

74. The word "red" is _____（有趣的）connected with feelings.

75. When _____（装修）rooms, they often disagreed with each other.

第二节　词形变换：用括号内单词的适当形式填空，将正确答案写在答题卡上相应题号后的横线上。（共5分，每小题1分）

76. Generally _____ (speak), Chinese food is good in taste, color and smell.

77. Seeing so many hungry persons makes them _____ (pleasant).

78. Hearing the news that their team won the match, the boys jumped with _____ (enjoy).

79. Calming colors can _____ (easy) people's emotion.

80. The foreigners were given a red-carpeted _____ (treat).

第三节 改错:从 A、B、C、D 四个画线处找出一处错误的选项填入答题卡上相应题号后的括号内,并在横线上写出正确答案。(共 10 分,每小题 2 分)

81. Old although he is, the driver is interested in learning English.
     A   B   C   D

82. In the whole, we are very satisfied with the operation.
   A   B   C   D

83. The old worker has warned you of the danger, didn't he?
              A   B   C   D

84. The young man was often associated to a famous hero.
         A   B   C   D

85. I don't know what profession would be suitable to him.
 A   B   C   D

81. (　　) 应为_____　　82. (　　) 应为_____

83. (　　) 应为_____　　84. (　　) 应为_____

85. (　　) 应为_____

第四节 书面表达。(共 10 分)

作文题目:What Is Most Important?

词数要求:80～100 词。

写作要点:1.每个人所重视的东西有所不同。

         2.你认为什么最重要。

Unit 5 Good Manners

单元基础知识闯关小测验

I. 汉译英。

1. 熟悉……_____   2. 在日常生活中_____

3. 发脾气_____   4. 羞于……_____

5. 后悔做了……_____   6. 为……而表示道歉_____

7. 换句话说_____   8. 不再;再也不_____

II. 词形变换。

1. convenience _____（反义词） 2. understandable _____（动词）

3. apologize _____（名词） 4. employee _____（动词）

5. similarly _____（形容词） 6. seldom _____（反义词）

III. 用 one, none, few, a few, little, a little 填空。

1. Stay away from this. It's _____ of your business.

2. We may get on well with a number of people, but we usually make friends with only _____ of them.

3. —Would you like some water?
   —Yes. Just _____.

4. There are very _____ chairs in the room. You'd better take _____ with you.

5. Hurry up! There is _____ time left.

单元综合练习

★★★

第一节 语音知识：从 A、B、C、D 四个选项中找出其画线部分与所给单词画线部分读音相同的选项。

( ) 1. for<u>g</u>ive   A. dama<u>g</u>e   B. apolo<u>g</u>y   C. chan<u>g</u>e   D. reco<u>g</u>nize

( ) 2. f<u>a</u>miliar   A. sh<u>a</u>me   B. dis<u>a</u>ppear   C. f<u>a</u>mous   D. l<u>a</u>ke

( ) 3. <u>a</u>ction   A. <u>a</u>dult   B. <u>a</u>dmire   C. <u>a</u>dvice   D. <u>a</u>pparent

( ) 4. sh<u>ou</u>t   A. y<u>ou</u>   B. gr<u>ou</u>p   C. s<u>ou</u>l   D. d<u>ou</u>bt

( ) 5. wonder<u>ed</u>   A. enter<u>ed</u>   B. need<u>ed</u>   C. want<u>ed</u>   D. develop<u>ed</u>

第二节 词汇与语法知识：从 A、B、C、D 四个选项中选出可以填入空白处的最佳选项。

( ) 1. In our _____, we sometimes say or do something that may hurt others.
     A. life   B. living   C. lived   D. lives

( ) 2. Making an _____ helps to mend a damaged relationship.
     A. apologize   B. apologized   C. apology   D. apologizes

( ) 3. They are familiar _____ each other.
     A. with   B. to   C. of   D. for

( ) 4. All the music played at yesterday's party was familiar _____ us.
     A. with   B. to   C. of   D. for

( ) 5. It might be worth _____ about.
     A. thinking   B. to think   C. thought   D. thoughts

( ) 6. He lost his temper and shouted _____ me.
     A. of   B. to   C. at   D. for

( ) 7. I must apologize _____ calling so late.
     A. to   B. by   C. for   D. of

( ) 8. Generally _____ ,I think you are right.
     A. speak   B. to speak   C. spoken   D. speaking

( ) 9. This is the best play _____ was written by Jack.
     A. that   B. which   C. he   D. who

50

Unit 5 Good Manners

(　　)10. I was _____ to go to bed when the telephone rang.
　　A. about　　　B. afraid　　　C. going　　　D. willing

(　　)11. John is recognized _____ the best soccer in the school.
　　A. to　　　B. for　　　C. with　　　D. as

(　　)12. _____ to his help, we finished the task early.
　　A. thank　　　B. Thanks　　　C. Thanking　　　D. Thank

(　　)13. —How many sisters do you have?
　　—I have only _____.
　　A. two　　　B. three　　　C. one　　　D. four

(　　)14. —Who is in the next room?
　　—_____.
　　A. No one　　　B. None　　　C. Nothing　　　D. Nobody

(　　)15. She will come to see me _____ next week.
　　A. some times　　B. sometime　　C. sometimes　　D. some time

(　　)16. Seldom _____, she is usually too sad.
　　A. does Mary smile
　　B. is Mary smile
　　C. Mary smiles
　　D. Mary smiled

(　　)17. Mr Wang _____ finished the work on time, because he has been in hospital for two months.
　　A. ought to　　B. couldn't have　　C. must have　　D. shall have

(　　)18. If you can't answer such a simple question, you'll _____ in class.
　　A. lost your face
　　B. lose a lot of face
　　C. lose your face
　　D. lose faces

(　　)19. Wood _____ often _____ tables.
　　A. is... used to making
　　B. are... used to make
　　C. are... used to making
　　D. is... used to make

(　　)20. The weather _____ good _____ bad.
　　A. vary from... to　B. varies... to　C. vary... to　D. varies from... to

第三节　完形填空:阅读下面的短文,从所给的 A、B、C、D 四个选项中选出最佳的答案。

　　Waste can be seen everywhere in the school. Some students ask for __1__ food than they can eat and others often forget __2__ off the lights when they leave the classroom.

They say they can afford these things. But I don't agree __3__ them.

Waste can bring a lot of __4__. __5__ China is rich in some resources, we are short of others, for example, fresh water. It's reported that we will have no coal or oil to use in 100 years. So if we go on __6__ our resources, what can we use in the future and where can we move? Think about it. I think we should say "no" to the students __7__ waste things every day. Everybody should stop wasting as soon as possible.

In our everyday life, we can do many things __8__ waste from happening, for example, turn __9__ the water taps when we finish washing, turn off the lights when we leave the classroom, try not to order more food __10__ we need, and so on. Little by little, everything will be changed. Waste can be stopped one day, if we do our best.

( )1. A. many   B. much   C. most   D. more
( )2. A. to turn   B. turning   C. turned   D. turns
( )3. A. to   B. with   C. on   D. for
( )4. A. questions   B. matters   C. problems   D. events
( )5. A. However   B. Although   C. But   D. While
( )6. A. waste   B. to waste   C. wasted   D. wasting
( )7. A. who   B. what   C. which   D. when
( )8. A. prevent   B. preventing   C. to prevent   D. prevented
( )9. A. off   B. on   C. to   D. back
( )10. A. when   B. what   C. than   D. while

第四节　阅读理解：阅读下列短文，从每题所给 A、B、C、D 四个选项中，选出最恰当的答案。

The E-schoolbag

Is your schoolbag too heavy to bear? The e-schoolbag will free you from the weight.

It is said that the e-schoolbags are going to be brought into use in Chinese middle schools soon. A trial project with several hundred e-schoolbags will begin in seven cities: Beijing, Shanghai, Dalian, Shenzhen, Chongqing, Shijiazhuang and Taiyuan.

A lucky class of students from each city will be first to use the e-schoolbags. The e-schoolbags are going to cover all over China if the trial project shows to be successful.

In fact, the e-schoolbag should perhaps be called an e-textbook. It is a small hand held computer for school students.

Heavy schoolbags have long been a serious problem for students. The average schoolbag of middle school students weighs up to five kilos. But the e-schoolbag will change everything. It is much lighter than a usual schoolbag, weighing under one kilo.

Also, it is no bigger than a usual book, but it can still hold all the things for study, such as a textbook, a notebook and an exercise book. They could be made into chips that are as small as a stamp. When the teacher asks the students to read the text, they will put the right chip into the e-schoolbag and read the text page by page on the screen.

Students can still take notes using a special electronic pen. If they want to know the meaning or the pronunciation of a new word, or even e-mail their teachers, it's just a press of a button.

In some foreign countries, the e-textbooks are becoming common. The United States and Singapore have begun to use e-textbooks in some schools. But it is hard to tell when people will receive this new form of study.

Some say that e-textbooks can easily be broken if a drink is knocked over on the desk. Some say that it is no good to students' eyesight to look at the screen for long. But only time will tell.

(　　)1. An e-schoolbag is _____.

　　A. too light to carry　　　　B. a small computer

　　C. no bigger than a stamp　　D. as cheap as an electronic pen

(　　)2. E-schoolbags are used for _____.

　　A. playing computer games　　B. computer studies

　　C. learning foreign languages　　D. school study

(　　)3. E-schoolbags _____.

　　A. are popular with all the people

　　B. can do everything for the students

　　C. may be used instead of usual schoolbags

　　D. will be easily received by people

(　　)4. A trial project with several hundred e-schoolbags will begin in _____.

　　A. Shanghai, Tianjin, Shijiazhuang

　　B. Dalian, Hebei, Shandong

C. Taiyuan, Hong Kong, Sichuan

D. Beijing, Chongqing, Taiyuan

(   )5. In some foreign countries, the e-textbook is becoming _____.

A. usual and ordinary　　　　　　B. rare

C. unusual　　　　　　　　　　　D. useful

第五节　词义搭配:从(B)栏中选出(A)栏单词的正确解释。

　　　　(A)　　　　　　　　　　(B)

(　)1. ashamed　　　　　　A. connection

(　)2. chance　　　　　　　B. well-known

(　)3. relationship　　　　　C. opportunity

(　)4. doubt　　　　　　　D. feel uncertain about something

(　)5. familiar　　　　　　　E. feeling very sorry and embarrassed

第六节　补全对话:根据对话内容,从对话后的选项中选出能填入空白处的最佳选项。

A: Excuse me, can you do me a favor?

B: Yes, of course. __1__

A: __2__

B: When and where did you last use it?

A: I made a call to my friend when I left my room for lunch, and then I came back to find it lost.

B: __3__

A: OK. I hope it will be found quickly. You know, I'm really worried about it.

B: __4__ Once we get the news, we'll inform you as soon as possible. Please don't worry. __5__

A: Yes. George, Room 222, sorry to trouble you.

B: You are welcome.

A. I'll call the Lost and Found Department immediately.

B. May I have your name and room number?

C. What's the matter with you, sir?

D. All right. We'll try our best to find it.

E. I can't find my mobile phone.

Unit 5 Good Manners

第七节 单词拼写。

1. You should be _____（害羞）of your bad manners.

2. He has a _____（机会）to go abroad.

3. If you are in _____（疑问）, you'd better not do it.

4. No one can avoid _____（犯）mistakes in their whole life.

5. She _____（认出）me in the street even if I was wearing a pair of sunglasses.

第八节 词形变换。

1. Peter was late, but his excuse sounded _____（understand）.

2. We apologized for the delay and any _____（convenient）.

3. Our relationship has _____（strong）over the years.

4. The _____（damage）house has been rebuilt.

5. You should make an _____（apologize）when you do something wrong.

第九节 改错：从 A、B、C、D 四个画线处找出一处错误的选项填入括号内，并在横线上写出正确答案。

1. A young girl dressing in black came into the room quickly.
   A   B   C   D

2. Had a high fever, he had to stay in bed.
   A   B   C   D

3. It is no use to argue with Mary to make her go there.
        A   B   C   D

4. They found it difficult finish the project in two days.
       A   B   C   D

5. This room is three times as bigger as that one.
         A   B   C D

1.（　　）应为_____   2.（　　）应为_____

3.（　　）应为_____   4.（　　）应为_____

5.（　　）应为_____

第十节 作文。

近年来，随着人们生活水平的提高，出国旅游的人数越来越多，但是，有一些人的不文明行为引起了人们的关注：随地吐痰，乱扔垃圾，乱涂乱画，大声喧哗，等车就餐不排队，不遵守交通规则等。请你根据这些要点，提出自己的意见和建议，写一篇 100 词左右的短文，涵盖上述要点，可以适当发挥。

参考词汇：spit(吐痰), behavior(行为)。

Unit 6 Chinese Heritage

单元基础知识闯关小测验

I. 汉译英。

1. 起源于_____
2. 以……为特征_____
3. 回溯到_____
4. 和……一样_____
5. 根据……的指示_____
6. 伴随；陪伴_____
7. 由……组成_____
8. 相当于；等于_____

II. 词形变换。

1. perform _____（名词）
2. combine _____（名词）
3. music _____（形容词）
4. character _____（动词）
5. humor _____（形容词）
6. indication _____（动词）

III. 用括号中词的适当形式填空。

1. You'll fail _____ (pass) the exam if you don't study hard.
2. The students couldn't help _____ (laugh) when they heard the joke.
3. Peter was pretending _____ (read) the book when the teacher came in.
4. Would you mind _____ (turn) down the music? The baby is sleeping.
5. She suggested _____ (try) once more.
6. We should practise _____ (speak) English every day.

单元综合练习

——★★★——

第一节 语音知识:从 A、B、C、D 四个选项中找出其画线部分与所给单词画线部分读音相同的选项。

( )1. arrange A. large B. market C. artist D. arrival

( )2. disaster A. star B. choose C. stage D. source

( )3. wood A. foot B. food C. flood D. blood

( )4. through A. though B. although C. theory D. these

( )5. state A. nature B. action C. admire D. actor

第二节 词汇与语法知识:从 A、B、C、D 四个选项中选出可以填入空白处的最佳选项。

( )1. The story dates back _____ the 19th century.

 A. as B. from C. to D. B and C

( )2. A friend is someone that you can rely _____.

 A. in B. of C. on D. to

( )3. We have _____ in common with each other.

 A. no B. not C. nothing D. none

( )4. The actors are _____ the film—Amazing China.

 A. performing B. performed C. performance D. performer

( )5. _____ as China's national opera, Beijing Opera originated in the late 18th century.

 A. Knowing B. Known C. To know D. Knows

( )6. Famous male actors _____ Tan Xinpei, Yang Xiaolou and Zhou Xinfang.

 A. include B. includes C. including D. has included

( )7. The snow _____ by a strong wind.

 A. accompany   B. accompanying

 C. was accompanied D. accompanies

( )8. The leading role in this play _____ by Gong Li.

 A. playing B. plays C. played D. is played

( )9. Our headmaster could not attend the meeting, so Mr Green _____ him.

    A. represent   B. represents   C. represented   D. representing

( )10. Sichuan food _____ by its spicy flavor.

    A. is characterized   B. characterized

    C. is charactered   D. characterize

( )11. The film is based _____ a real story.

    A. at   B. on   C. of   D. with

( )12. Our class _____ 20 boy students and 26 girl students.

    A. consist of   B. consists of

    C. is consisted of   D. is consisting of

( )13. _____ money, he's rich, but not happy.

    A. To terms of   B. In terms of

    C. At terms of   D. With terms of

( )14. They insisted a doctor _____ at once.

    A. be sent for   B. sent for   C. is sending for   D. sended for

( )15. _____ there is water, there is life.

    A. If   B. That   C. When   D. Where

( )16. Leave the things _____ they are.

    A. which   B. when   C. as   D. for

( )17. Clouds _____ the coming of rain.

    A. indicates   B. indicate   C. indicating   D. are indicated

( )18. Beijing Opera has become an elegant art form _____ the hard work of hundreds of artists over the past two centuries.

    A. for result   B. as a result,   C. as a result   D. as a result of

( )19. These forces oppose each other and at the same time _____ each other.

    A. complement   B. complete   C. completed   D. completely

( )20. She regards my friend _____ respect.

    A. at   B. with   C. for   D. as

Unit 6 Chinese Heritage

第三节 完形填空:阅读下面的短文,从所给的 A、B、C、D 四个选项中选出最佳的答案。

Because of an apple that shouldn't have dropped, a child is destroyed. A family is also __1__. This scary apple, __2__ to the innocent(无辜的) family, but also to our whole society, is a kind of unbearable(不可承受的) pain.

Tragedies(悲剧) __3__ by throwing things in the high sky __4__ in a great number. However it repeats, becoming a public hazard(危险). __5__ things from upstairs __6__ "a threat hanging over a city." It happens a lot and can't __7__. It is a time bomb which is __8__ threaten to security(安全) and a difficult point for monitoring(监控).

The action is greatly __9__. Throwing a 300g egg from the eighth floor can cut a person's scalp(头皮). __10__ from the 18th floor, it can break a person's skull(头骨). And it can kill a person if from the 25th floor. Please don't throw anything from upstairs.

( )1. A. destroy   B. destroys   C. to destroy   D. destroyed
( )2. A. not   B. not only   C. for   D. because
( )3. A. caused   B. causing   C. are caused   D. is caused
( )4. A. is   B. are   C. was   D. were
( )5. A. Throwing   B. Thrown   C. To throw   D. Threw
( )6. A. are called B. called   C. is called   D. calling
( )7. A. stopped   B. being stopped C. stop   D. be stopped
( )8. A. the   B. a   C. an   D. /
( )9. A. harmful   B. harm   C. harmless   D. to harm
( )10. A. When   B. Unless   C. If   D. Because

第四节 阅读理解:阅读下列短文,从每题所给 A、B、C、D 四个选项中,选出最恰当的答案。

According to court documents, Rohana was attending an "Ugly Sweater Party" at the Franklin Institute on December 21th last year (2017) when he made his way into the Terracotta Warriors（兵马俑）exhibition, which was then closed. He then put his hand on the left hand of the statue and appeared to break something off from it. He pocketed the item and left.

Museum staff noticed the missing thumb on January 8th this year and the FBI later traced (追踪) it to Rohana. He later admitted that he had kept the thumb in a desk drawer.

The Shanxi Cultural Heritage Promotion Center said it had organized more than 260 overseas exhibitions in the past 40 years and had never come across such a situation before.

(　　)1. Who stole the thumb of the statue?

　　A. FBI.　　　　B. Museum staff.　　C. Rohana.　　　D. The lawyer.

(　　)2. When did the theft happen?

　　A. On December 21th, 2017.　　　B. On January 8th, 2018.

　　C. In the past 40 years.　　　　D. Not mentioned in the passage.

(　　)3. What was Rohana doing at the Franklin Institute at that time?

　　A. He was drinking coffee.　　　B. He was visiting.

　　C. He was passing by.　　　　D. He was attending a party.

(　　)4. The passage is mainly about _____.

　　A. The Shanxi Cultural Heritage Promotion Center organized 260 overseas exhibitions in the past 40 years

　　B. Rohana attended an "Ugly Sweater Party" at the Franklin Institute

　　C. The thumb of Chinese Terracotta Warrior Statues was stolen

　　D. Rohana made his way into the Terracotta Warriors (兵马俑) exhibit

(　　)5. The conclusion we can get from the passage is _____.

　　A. The Shanxi Cultural Heritage Promotion Center will not hold the exhibition

　　B. Rohana will be punished by the law

　　C. Rohana won't attend the "Ugly Sweater Party"

　　D. Rohana won't be punished by the law

第五节　词义搭配：从(B)栏中选出(A)栏单词的正确解释。

　　　　(A)　　　　　　　　　(B)

(　　)1. leading　　　A. act/speak for sb.

(　　)2. force　　　　B. stupid

(　　)3. represent　　C. character

( )4. silly   D. make sb. do something that they don't want to do

( )5. personality   E. most important or most successful

第六节 补全对话：根据对话内容，从对话后的选项中选出能填入空白处的最佳选项。

A：Good evening, ladies and gentlemen. Welcome to our restaurant.

B：__1__

A：Did you have a reservation, sir?

B：No.

A：__2__ Would you mind waiting for a moment?

B：How long?

A：Maybe about fifteen minutes. __3__

B：It doesn't matter. We have plenty of time.

A：OK. __4__

B：Thanks a lot.

A：__5__ Please have a seat here. Sorry for the delay.

B：Great!

A. Sorry, sir. All our tables are taken.

B. If you are in a hurry, we also offer snacks at the coffee shop on the first floor.

C. We'll arrange a table for you as soon as possible.

D. We can arrange your seats now, sir.

E. Good evening. Is there a table for seven people?

第七节 单词拼写。

1. Beijing Opera is an important part of the Chinese _____ (文化).

2. Walking in a circle around the _____ (舞台) indicates a long journey.

3. Mary is in a red coat and looks very _____ (有吸引力的).

4. _____ (传统的) Chinese medicine is unique because of its special methods of treatment.

5. This kind of treatment aims at readjusting the _____ (平衡) in a person's body.

第八节 词形变换。

1. _____ (medicine) conditions in our country are improving.

2. You can't be _____ (independent) on your parents all your life.

3. Children are highly adaptable — they just need time to _____ (adjust).

4. He is so _____ (humor) that we all love him.

5. The _____ (important) of studying English is well-known.

第九节 改错：从 A、B、C、D 四个画线处找出一处错误的选项填入括号内，并在横线上写出正确答案。

1. You'd better to avoid reading in the bus.
    A   B   C   D

2. I'm determined giving up smoking.
       A   B   C   D

3. He prefers watching TV to play basketball.
     A   B   C   D

4. In Beijing Opera there are four types of role.
   A   B   C   D

5. Symbol is very important in Beijing Opera.
   A   B   C   D

1. (　　) 应为 _____   2. (　　) 应为 _____

3. (　　) 应为 _____   4. (　　) 应为 _____

5. (　　) 应为 _____

第十节 作文。

作文题目：The Popular E-card。

词数要求：100 个词左右。

写作要点：1. 介绍电子贺卡的优越性。

2. 可传播动画（animation）和声音。

3. 传递速度快。

4. 形式多样。

5. 节省人力（man-power）和资金。

6. 有利于环境保护。

阶段测试题(Unit 5~Unit 6)

第一部分 英语知识运用

（共分三节，满分40分）

——★★★——

第一节 语音知识：从A、B、C、D四个选项中找出其画线部分与所给单词画线部分读音相同的选项，并在答题卡上将该项涂黑。（共5分，每小题1分）

( )1. si_g_nal   A. l_i_on   B. si_g_n   C. reco_g_nize   D. i_n_dicate

( )2. dou_b_t   A. _b_oss   B. cli_m_b   C. _b_ase   D. distur_b_

( )3. _th_eory   A. bo_th_   B. _th_ose   C. _th_ere   D. _th_us

( )4. m_e_tal   A. forc_e_   B. sh_e_   C. m_e_dicine   D. m_e_

( )5. m_a_ss   A. _a_ctor   B. _a_bility   C. _a_dapt   D. _a_ffect

第二节 词汇与语法知识：从A、B、C、D四个选项中选出可以填入空白处的最佳选项，并在答题卡上将该项涂黑。（共25分，每小题1分）

( )6. —Hurry up! Here _____! Where is Cindy?
　　—There _____.
　　A. comes the train; is she　　　B. comes the train; she is
　　C. the train comes; is she　　　D. the train comes; she is

( )7. I will try _____ best to study English well.
　　A. one's　　B. mine　　C. me　　D. my

( )8. The old lady managed _____ the mountain.
　　A. to climb　　B. climb　　C. climbing　　D. climbed

( )9. The house needs _____.
　　A. repair　　B. repairing　　C. to repair　　D. repaired

( )10. This car can only work _____ sunny days.

　　A. in　　　　B. at　　　　C. on　　　　D. of

( )11. I regret _____ I haven't given you enough help.

　　A. to say　　B. saying　　C. said　　D. say

( )12. When the teacher came in, the students stopped _____ at once.

　　A. talk　　　B. talked　　C. to talk　　D. talking

( )13. She told me not to leave the window _____.

　　A. closed　　B. to be closed　　C. to close　　D. closing

( )14. Seldom _____ hear the father say "I'm sorry" to his son.

　　A. did we　　B. we did　　C. we do　　D. do we

( )15. Now more and more people have a better _____ of apologizing.

　　A. understand　　B. understanding　　C. understood　　D. understands

( )16. The apology _____ barriers to communication and strengthen a mutual relationship.

　　A. is used to removing　　　　B. used to removed

　　C. is used to remove　　　　 D. used to remove

( )17. Are you familiar _____ these expressions for greetings?

　　A. to　　　　B. of　　　　C. with　　　　D. at

( )18. I don't like the way _____ you treat me.

　　A. /　　　　B. which　　　　C. for　　　　D. if

( )19. You must apologize _____ me _____ here.

　　A. to; for didn't come　　　　B. to; for not coming

　　C. with; for not coming　　　 D. with; for not to come

( )20. I have _____.

　　A. something important will do　　B. something important to be done

　　C. important something to do　　　D. something important to do

( )21. He felt ashamed _____ the exam.

　　A. of not passing　　B. of not to pass　　C. of passing　　D. for passing

( )22. He asked me _____.

　　A. where did it happen　　B. how did it happen

　　C. where it happens　　　 D. how it happened

( )23. It's not polite to _____ those who are disabled.

· 64 ·

A. laugh to　　B. laugh at　　C. smile at　　D. smile to

(　)24. The old man enjoyed _____ the children _____ basketball.

　　A. to watch; to play　　　　B. watching; played

　　C. watching; playing　　　　D. to watch; playing

(　)25. _____ fine weather it is!

　　A. What　　B. What a　　C. How　　D. How a

(　)26. —Would you mind my opening the window?

　　—_____.

　　A. You'd better not　　　　B. Sorry, you can't.

　　C. Yes, please　　　　　　D. Yes, you can.

(　)27. —She went to see the film last night.

　　—_____.

　　A. So I did　　B. So I was　　C. So was I　　D. So did I

(　)28. _____ more time, we will finish the work on time.

　　A. To give　　B. Given　　C. Giving　　D. Gave

(　)29. The reason _____ she was late for the meeting was _____ her bike was broken.

　　A. that; why　　B. why; that　　C. why; which　　D. because; that

(　)30. People are often _____ by weather and colors.

　　A. effected　　B. affect　　C. moved　　D. affected

第三节　完形填空:阅读下面的短文,从所给的每组 A、B、C、D 四个选项中选择正确的答案,并在答题卡上将该项涂黑。(共10分,每小题1分)

　　Once a gentleman was travelling on a train. He felt __31__ and got off at a station. When he reached the water tap, the train started. He missed it.

　　It was getting __32__, he decided to find a place for a day's __33__.

　　At last he reached a small house. He asked the owner __34__ he could stay here for a day. The owner immediately __35__, then served him food and gave him a room to stay. But he did not ask anything in return(作为回报).

　　At seven, the gentleman saw a man dressed in __36__ clothes enter the house and asked the owner to pay his debts(债务).

　　The gentleman came to know that the owner was in need of __37__. The next

65

morning he left a pack in the room and went away. When the owner found the pack, he saw that there was a note __38__ to him, which read: "You helped me __39__ did not expect anything from me. Yesterday evening I heard the conversation between you and the stranger. This is __40__ you need."

( )31. A. sleepy   B. happy   C. thirsty   D. tired
( )32. A. cold   B. dark   C. hot   D. bright
( )33. A. work   B. travel   C. fun   D. stay
( )34. A. how   B. why   C. whether   D. when
( )35. A. agreed   B. received   C. accepted   D. refused
( )36. A. cheaper   B. strange   C. expensive   D. dirty
( )37. A. advice   B. money   C. time   D. water
( )38. A. to write   B. wrote   C. being written   D. written
( )39. A. but   B. and   C. so   D. if
( )40. A. what   B. that   C. which   D. when

第二部分　篇章与词汇理解

（共分三节，满分50分）

——★★★——

第一节　阅读理解：阅读下列短文，从每题所给A、B、C、D四个选项中，选出最恰当的答案，并在答题卡上将该项涂黑。（共30分，每小题2分）

A

Jack Hawkins was the football <u>coach</u> at an American college, and he was always trying to find good players, but they were not always smart enough to be accepted by the college.

One day, the coach brought an excellent young player to the dean of the college and suggested that the student should be allowed to enter the college without an examination. "Well," the dean said after some persuasion, "I'd better ask him a few questions first."

Then he turned to the student and asked him some very easy questions, but the student didn't know any of the answers.

At last, the dean said, "Well, what's five times seven?"

The student thought for a long time and then answered,"Thirty-six."

The dean threw up his hands and looked at the coach in despair,but the coach said earnestly,"Oh,please let him in,sir! He was only wrong by two."

( )41. The word "coach" in Para. 1 means _____.

  A. a person who is good at drawing pictures

  B. a person who often rides horse

  C. someone who trains a person or team in a sport

  D. a bus driver

( )42. The coach thought five times seven is _____.

  A. thirty-four B. thirty-six C. thirty-eight D. thirty-five

( )43. Which of the following is TRUE according to the passage?

  A. The student is very clever.

  B. The coach is very clever.

  C. The student is as clever as the coach.

  D. Both of the student and the coach are not clever.

( )44. What can you learn from the passage?

  A. The student was accepted by the college.

  B. The dean didn't allow the student to enter the college.

  C. The student went abroad.

  D. The student was very angry.

( )45. The best title of the passage is _____.

  A. A Clever Student B. A Clever Coach

  C. A Clever Dean D. He Was Only Wrong by Two.

B

During my second year of nursing school,our professor gave us a quiz. I breezed through the questions until I read the last one,"What is the first name of the woman who cleans the school?" Surely this was a joke. I had seen the cleaning woman several times,but how could I know her name? I handed in my paper,leaving the last question blank.

Before the class ended,one student asked if the last question would count towards our grade. "Absolutely," the professor said. "In your careers, you will meet many people. All are significant. They deserve your attention and care,even if all you do is smile and say hello."

I've never forgotten the valuable lesson. I also learned her name was Dorothy.

(   )46. What is the meaning of the word "deserve" in Para. 2?

  A. 值得.　　　　B. 接受.　　　　C. 沙漠.　　　　D. 为……服务.

(   )47. What did the writer think of the questions?

  A. The writer thought some questions were easy while others were difficult.

  B. The writer thought all the questions were easy except the last one.

  C. The writer thought all the questions were easy.

  D. The writer thought all the questions were difficult.

(   )48. The best title of the passage is _____.

  A. What the Professor Teaches　　　B. A Quiz

  C. A Cleaning Woman　　　　　　D. My Professor

(   )49. Which of the following is TRUE according to the passage?

  A. The cleaning woman has no name.

  B. The professor's name is Dorothy.

  C. The cleaning woman's name is Dorothy.

  D. The writer's name is Dorothy.

(   )50. What is the main idea of this passage?

  A. Only your classmates deserve your attention care.

  B. Only your professor deserves your attention and care.

  C. people who you met or you will meet are not important in your careers.

  D. Many people who you met or you will meet deserve your attention and care.

C

More and more students want to study in "hot" majors. As a result, many students want to give up their interests and study in these areas, such as foreign languages, international business and law, etc. Fewer and fewer students choose scientific majors, such as math, physics and biology, and art majors, like history, Chinese and philosophy (哲学). Only a few students can study in these "hot" majors, because the number of these "hot" majors is limited.

If one has no interest in his work or study, how can he do well? I heard this from one of my classmates, he is from the countryside, his parents are farmers. Though he likes biology, he chose "international business." He wants to live a life which is different from that of his parents. In the end, he found he was not interested in doing business. He found all the subjects to be tiresome. Maybe this wouldn't have happened if he had chosen his major according to his own interests.

Choosing a major in university doesn't decide one's whole life. Majors which are not "hot" today may become the "hot" majors of tomorrow. Choosing your major according to your own interests is the best way to succeed.

(　　)51. According to the passage, "hot" majors include the following except _____.

　　A. laws　　　　　　　　　　B. foreign languages

　　C. international business　　　D. history

(　　)52. Why can only a few students study in these "hot" majors?

　　A. Because these "hot" majors are very popular.

　　B. Because only a few students can give up their interests.

　　C. Because the number of these "hot" majors is limited.

　　D. Because many students don't want to study in these "hot" majors.

(　　)53. Who can study in the "hot" majors?

　　A. All the students can study in these "hot" majors.

　　B. Only a few students can study in these "hot" majors.

　　C. Only the boy students can study in these "hot" majors.

　　D. Only the students from the countryside can study in these "hot" majors.

(　　)54. In choosing your major in university, what should you do according to the passage?

　　A. You should choose your major according to your own interests.

　　B. You should give up your interests.

　　C. You should follow your parents' advice.

　　D. You should follow your teachers' advice.

(　　)55. Which of the following is true about the "hot" majors?

　　A. Majors that are not "hot" today may become the "hot" majors of tomorrow.

　　B. Today's "hot" majors will be "hot" forever.

　　C. Choosing a "hot" major in a university decides one's whole life.

　　D. The "hot" majors will disappear.

第二节　词义搭配:从(B)栏中选出(A)栏单词的正确解释,并在答题卡上将该项涂黑。(共10分,每小题1分)

(A)	(B)
(　　)56. originate	A. showing a sense of humour
(　　)57. frequent	B. to watch sb./sth. carefully
(　　)58. technique	C. to show that sth. is true or exists
(　　)59. accompany	D. happening or doing sth. often
(　　)60. disaster	E. a sudden event which causes great damage
(　　)61. humorous	F. a request for information
(　　)62. indicate	G. to go somewhere with someone
(　　)63. observe	H. to know who sb. is
(　　)64. inquiry	I. a special way of doing something
(　　)65. recognize	J. to happen or appear for the first time in a place

第三节　补全对话:根据对话内容,从对话后的选项中选出能填入空白处的最佳选项,并在答题卡上将该项涂黑。(共10分,每小题2分)

A:Good afternoon! Welcome to Hainan Hotel. May I help you?

B:Yes, __66__

A:Certainly, sir. __67__

B:I'm Brown.

A: __68__

B:Yes, from tonight.

A:Just a moment please. I'll check our reservation record... Thank you for waiting, Mr Brown. __69__ Is that right?

B:Exactly.

A:Could you fill out the registration form, please?

B:Fine. (Fill out the form)

A: __70__

B:By credit card.

A:OK. Your room number is 2009. That's on the 8th floor. Please enjoy your stay here.

A. Do you have a reservation, Mr Brown?

B. How would you like to pay?

C. May I have your name, please?

D. I'd like to check in, please.

E. Your reservation is for a double room from March 5th to 7th for three nights.

第三部分　语言技能运用

（共分四节,满分30分）

———★★★———

第一节　单词拼写：根据下列句子及所给汉语注释,在答题卡上相应题号后的横线上写出该单词。（共5分,每小题1分）

71. How important is an _____（道歉）in personal relationship?

72. Learning how to apologize is important in interpersonal _____（交流）.

73. Please _____（接受）my invitation.

74. We should learn about Chinese _____（传统的）culture.

75. I feel great _____（后悔）for my mistakes.

第二节　词形变换：用括号内单词的适当形式填空,将正确答案写在答题卡上相应题号后的横线上。（共5分,每小题1分）

76. The new student made a good _____（express）on the teachers.

77. They _____（success）in passing the exam.

78. He is _____（friend）to us.

79. The boss dismissed the lazy _____（employ）.

80. I'm sorry it is not _____（avail）today. Would you please come tomorrow?

第三节　改错：从A、B、C、D四个画线处找出一处错误的选项填入答题卡上相应题号后的括号内,并在横线上写出正确答案。（共10分,每小题2分）

81. Mr. Wang will have his watch repair.
　　　A　　　B　C　　　　D

82. <u>Only</u> <u>in this way</u> <u>you can</u> study English <u>well</u>.
　　 A　　　　B　　　　　C　　　　　　　 D

83. <u>Passengers</u> <u>are</u> <u>requested</u> <u>showing</u> <u>their</u> ID cards.
　　　　A　　　　　　　　B　　　　C　　　　D

84. I <u>apologize</u> <u>to</u> <u>my</u> poor <u>attitude</u>.
　　　　　A　　　 B　　C　　　　　D

85. <u>Learn</u> <u>how to</u> use the computer <u>is</u> very <u>important</u>.
　　　A　　　　　B　　　　　　　　　　 C　　　　D

81. (　　) 应为_____　　　　　82. (　　) 应为_____

83. (　　) 应为_____　　　　　84. (　　) 应为_____

85. (　　) 应为_____

第四节　书面表达。(共10分)

作文题目：The Great Changes in My Hometown。

词数要求：80～100词。

写作要点：1. 重点写出家乡新的变化。

　　　　　2. 体现出对家乡的热爱。

　　　　　3. 题目和开头已经给出，不计入词数。

　　　　　4. 参考词汇：used to be；take place；be covered by；newly born。

<h3 style="text-align:center">The Great Changes in My Hometown</h3>

With the development of economy, great changes have **taken place** in my hometown.

期中综合测试题

第一部分 英语知识运用

（共分三节,满分40分）

第一节 语音知识:从 A、B、C、D 四个选项中找出其画线部分与所给单词画线部分读音相同的选项,并在答题卡上将该项涂黑。（共5分,每小题1分）

( )1. lost   A. lose   B. politely   C. communicate   D. involve
( )2. strengthen A. thanks   B. rather   C. although   D. without
( )3. choose   A. outlook   B. mood   C. foot   D. blood
( )4. attract   A. general   B. hate   C. attitude   D. annoy
( )5. reasonably A. jeans   B. instead   C. ready   D. greatly

第二节 词汇与语法知识:从 A、B、C、D 四个选项中选出可以填入空白处的最佳选项,并在答题卡上将该项涂黑。（共25分,每小题1分）

( )6. Which city has _____ larger population, Beijing or Shijiazhuang?
   A. a   B. an   C. the   D. /

( )7. Nobody can _____ the people who always tell lies.
   A. is tolerant of   B. be tolerant of
   C. is tolerant to   D. be tolerant to

( )8. I had some trouble _____ the book. There are too many new words.
   A. read   B. to read   C. reading   D. readed

( )9. We often express our thought _____ words.
   A. though   B. through   C. by means of   D. by mean of

( )10. If you can't solve the problem, you can _____ your teacher.
   A. turn on   B. turn to   C. turn   D. turn for

· 73 ·

(   )11. He _____ the conversation from one subject to another.
   A. switched to   B. switched on   C. switched off   D. switched

(   )12. —How have you been?
   —_____.
   A. Can't be good   B. Couldn't be good
   C. Can't be better   D. Couldn't be better

(   )13. _____ as he is, he always helps others.
   A. Child   B. A child   C. Children   D. The child

(   )14. Our teacher often speaks louder in class _____ he can be heard by all of us.
   A. so as to   B. in order to   C. so that   D. such that

(   )15. She was _____ protecting wild animals.
   A. involve in   B. involving   C. to involve in   D. involved in

(   )16. _____ his help, I can finish the work on time.
   A. For   B. Because   C. Thanks   D. Thanks to

(   )17. _____ something happens, he chooses an optimistic attitude.
   A. Each time   B. Each time when
   C. Each once   D. Each time which

(   )18. —Your brother is a very honest boy.
   —Yes, _____.
   A. so does he   B. so he does   C. so is he   D. so he is

(   )19. Children who like playing football often _____ their shoes very quickly.
   A. wear off   B. wear out   C. wear away   D. wear

(   )20. My mom likes to _____ beautiful dresses _____ colorful cloth.
   A. make; out of   B. be made; out of
   C. make; into   D. be made; into

(   )21. My bike is broken, I have to have it _____.
   A. repair   B. repairing   C. repaired   D. to repair

(   )22. The boy _____ Li Lei is my best friend.
   A. names   B. named   C. naming   D. be named

(   )23. When I got home, I found my mother _____ in bed sleeping.

A. lay	B. lie	C. lying	D. lain

( )24. The teacher came into the classroom _____ by two children.

  A. with   B. followed   C. following   D. was followed

( )25. _____ more time, I would do the job much better.

  A. Give   B. Giving   C. Gave   D. Given

( )26. The problem _____ at the meeting now is very important.

  A. being discussed   B. be discussed

  C. discussing   D. discussed

( )27. _____ from the top of the mountain, we can find the city more beautiful.

  A. Seen   B. Seeing   C. See   D. Saw

( )28. When _____ out in the US, we can ask for tea, milk, beer and so on.

  A. eating   B. ate   C. eat   D. eaten

( )29. The food which _____ sugar and salt is bad for your health.

  A. rich in   B. rich at   C. is rich in   D. is rich with

( )30. In a word, food _____ in American culture.

  A. play an important role   B. plays an important role

  C. play a important role   D. playing a important role

第三节 完形填空:阅读下面的短文,从所给的每组 A、B、C、D 四个选项中选择正确的答案,并在答题卡上将该项涂黑。(共 10 分,每小题 1 分)

  Good manners are very __31__ in the communication of daily life. Everyone likes a person __32__ good manners. But what are good manners? How does one know what should be done and what should not be done when __33__ to be a good-mannered person?

  Here are some common examples. A person with good manners __34__ laughs at people in trouble. Instead, he always tries to consult or offer help to the person. When he takes a bus and sees an old man or a sick man, he always gives his __35__ to him. He doesn't interrupt other people when they are talking. He uses a handkerchief when he __36__ or coughs. He does not spite in public places.

  Ideas of what are good manners are not always __37__ in different regions. For example, people in Western countries usually kiss each other __38__ their greetings, but

in China, kissing in public is something of unusual and sometimes be regarded as impolite to somebody else. So __39__ is important to know what is regarded as polite and impolite __40__ you go to a region. But remember that it is always right to be kind and helpful to others.

( )31. A. easy   B. hard   C. important   D. trouble
( )32. A. with   B. together   C. on   D. as well as
( )33. A. try   B. trying   C. to try   D. tried
( )34. A. often   B. always   C. usually   D. never
( )35. A. seat   B. bus   C. car   D. room
( )36. A. laughs   B. sneezes   C. cries   D. eats
( )37. A. same   B. the same   C. different   D. the different
( )38. A. show   B. showed   C. to show   D. shows
( )39. A. that   B. this   C. its   D. it
( )40. A. before   B. ago   C. after   D. as soon as

第二部分 篇章与词汇理解

（共分三节，满分50分）

——★★★——

第一节 阅读理解：阅读下列短文，从每题所给 A、B、C、D 四个选项中，选出最恰当的答案，并在答题卡上将该项涂黑。（共30分，每小题2分）

A

Look around and you'll see people busy on their smart phones. Smart phones do make our lives easier. But have you ever thought about what they mean to your eyes?

According to a study, half of British people own smart phones and they spend an average(平均) of two hours a day using them. There has been a 35% increase in the number of people in the UK who suffer from shortsightedness(近视) since smart phones were introduced there in 1997.

Staring(盯) at smart phones for a long time gives you dry eyes. When you look at something in the distance, your eyes automatically blink(自动眨眼) a certain number of times. However, when you look at things closer to your face, the blinking slows down. This reduces the amount of tears and causes discomfort in your eyes. Another bad habit

76

is using smart phones in dark rooms before going to sleep. If you look at bright screen while your pupils(瞳孔) become larger, too much light enters your eyes. This can do harm to the eyes and cause a disease called glaucoma(青光眼).

So in order to protect your eyes, you'd better hold your phone at least 30 centimeters away from your eyes when using it. Take a break every hour and try the following: look at something at least five meters from you and then focus on the tip of your nose.

( )41. Which of the following is right?

   A. Smart phones make our lives easier.

   B. The people who have phones must be shortsighted.

   C. It is not bad for your eyes staring at smart phones for a long time.

   D. Using smart phones in dark rooms is a good habit.

( )42. The second paragraph tells us _____.

   A. half of the British people began to use smart phones 17 years ago

   B. each of the British people spends 2 hours a day on smart phones

   C. the number of people owning smart phones increases by 35%

   D. more British people have got shortsightedness since 1997

( )43. Using smart phones improperly may cause _____.

   A. more tears in the eyes   B. too many blinks

   C. dry eyes and glaucoma   D. smaller pupils

( )44. Which of the following is suggested by the writer?

   A. Hold the phones at least 30cm away from your eyes.

   B. Take a rest every two hours.

   C. Turn off your phones ten hours a day.

   D. Not to buy a smart phone.

( )45. The passage is mainly about _____.

   A. the importance to buy a phone

   B. the advantages and disadvantages of smart phones

   C. the reason why teenagers get shortsightedness

   D. the harm that smart phones do to users' eyes

B

Once there was a poor farmer and his farm belonged to(属于) a rich man. One day

he brought a basket of apples to the rich man's house. On the doorsteps, he met two monkeys dressed like children. They jumped onto the basket to eat the apples and threw some on the ground. The farmer politely took off his hat and asked the monkeys to get off. They obeyed(服从) and the farmer went into the house. He asked to see the rich man. A servant took him to the room where the rich man was sitting.

"I have brought you the basket of apples you asked for," he said.

"But why have you brought a half-empty basket?" the rich man asked.

"I met your children outside, and they stole(偷) some of the apples."

(　　)46. Why did the farmer bring apples to the rich man? Because _____.
　　A. he was poor
　　B. he liked the rich man
　　C. his farm belonged to the rich man
　　D. the rich man's children liked apples

(　　)47. What did the monkeys do when the farmer was on the doorsteps?
　　A. They jumped and jumped.　　B. They played.
　　C. They ran away.　　D. They ate some of the apples.

(　　)48. The monkeys left the basket because _____.
　　A. they had thrown apples on the ground
　　B. the farmer had politely asked them to get off
　　C. they were afraid of the farmer
　　D. the farmer was angry with them

(　　)49. How did the rich man feel when he saw the basket? He felt _____.
　　A. pleased　　B. unhappy　　C. excited　　D. moved

(　　)50. Who stole the apples in the basket?
　　A. The farmer.　　B. The rich man.　　C. Two monkeys.　　D. Two children.

C

Once a boy came to ask a fisherman how to become cleverer, because his mother always called him "foolish boy."

"That's easy," answered the fisherman. "I know one way to make you become cleverer."

"Really?"

"Of course. It is said a fish head is good for brain. If you eat one, you'll become cleverer indeed. Pay only three pounds for one fish head." The boy paid him three pounds and the fisherman cut off a fish head and handed it to him.

A raw fish head is not good—not even for a hungry boy to eat but the boy ate it up in two gulps.

"Do you feel anything?" asked the fisherman.

"Not in my head," said the boy.

The boy lay on the ground and thought. "One whole fish costs only two pounds. I had paid him three pounds for the fish head. Why couldn't I have the whole fish for soup, a head for brain and one pound left over?" He jumped up and shouted at the fisherman. "You thief! You are fooling me!" The fisherman laughed, saying, "The fish head works now, you see."

( )51. The boy came to the fisherman in order to _____.

    A. buy a fish head   B. ask the fisherman a question

    C. buy a whole fish   D. A and C

( ) 52. The boy ate up the raw fish head only in two gulps, because he _____.

    A. enjoyed it   B. wanted to taste it

    C. took it as a good medicine   D. was a foolish boy

( )53. The boy paid three pounds. He should have had _____.

    A. a whole fish

    B. a fish head and one pound back

    C. a whole fish and one pound back

    D. a whole fish, a fish head and one pound back

( )54. _____ helped the boy become cleverer.

    A. A good meal   B. The raw fish head

    C. Nothing   D. What had happened

( )55. Which of the following is TRUE?

    A. The boy is really very foolish.

    B. The idea of the fisherman is not useful to the boy.

    C. The fish head can make a person more clever.

    D. The boy thanked the fisherman very much.

第二节 词义搭配:从(B)栏中选出(A)栏单词的正确解释,并在答题卡上将该项涂黑。(共10分,每小题1分)

(A)	(B)
(　)56. bottom	A. not like, consider unhappy
(　)57. optimistic	B. say or do something again
(　)58. annoy	C. confident expecting the best
(　)59. repeat	D. informal talk
(　)60. engage	E. make someone feel angry
(　)61. trousers	F. the lowest part of anything
(　)62. dislike	G. take part in
(　)63. intend	H. of different kinds
(　)64. conversation	I. pants
(　)65. various	J. plan, have in mind as a purpose

第三节 补全对话:根据对话内容,从对话后的选项中选出能填入空白处的最佳选项,并在答题卡上将该项涂黑。(共10分,每小题2分)

A:Excuse me. __66__?

B:Yes, you can take No. 5 bus there.

A: __67__?

B:Yes, it will take an hour and a half.

A:Oh, my god! __68__.

B:Then you'd better take a taxi.

A:A taxi? __69__.

B:Here comes a taxi.

A:Thanks a lot.

B: __70__. Goodbye!

A:Bye-bye!

> A. Yes, it's much faster.
> B. You are welcome.
> C. Could you tell me the way to the airport?
> D. Is it far from here?
> E. I have only an hour left.

第三部分 语言技能运用

（共分四节,满分30分）

——★★★——

第一节 单词拼写:根据下列句子及所给汉语注释,在答题卡上相应题号后的横线上写出该单词。（共5分,每小题1分）

71. Sorry, I can't _____ （解释）why I can't solve the problem.

72. With the help of my friends, I _____ （成功）in finishing the work.

73. The _____ （各种各样的）styles of clothes make people more beautiful.

74. Jake is an optimistic guy and he is always _____ （无忧无虑的）.

75. Narrow trousers are in _____ （时尚）nowadays.

第二节 词形变换:用括号内单词的适当形式填空,将正确答案写在答题卡上相应题号后的横线上。（共5分,每小题1分）

76. His two children always greet old people _____ (polite).

77. They _____ (strong) their friendship by doing the work together.

78. Choose the one you love and live _____ (happy) with him.

79. Chinese is our _____ (nation) language.

80. I lost my watch and I felt _____ (depress).

第三节 改错:从A、B、C、D四个画线处找出一处错误的选项填入答题卡上相应题号后的括号内,并在横线上写出正确答案。（共10分,每小题2分）

81. When I met her in the street, she pretended not seeing me.
　　　　　A　　　B　　　　　　　C　　　　D

82. I think Tom went to the tower yesterday, do I?
　　A　　　　B　　C　　　　　　　　D

83. The head of the factory explained the workers he had to close the factory
　　　　　　　　　　　　　　　　　A　　　　　　B
because of his illness.
　　C　　　　D

84. If you helped me at that time, I would have finished the task on time.
　　A　　B　　　　　　　　　C　　　　　　　　　　　　　D

85. The trousers were sold well and Strauss began looking around for materials of
　　　　　　　　　A　　　　　　　　　　　　　A
making new ones.
　　C　　　D

81. ( ) 应为_____ 82. ( ) 应为_____

83. ( ) 应为_____ 84. ( ) 应为_____

85. ( ) 应为_____

第四节 书面表达。(共 10 分)

作文题目:Attitude Towards Life。

词数要求:80~100 词。

写作要点:1.生活就是一次长途旅行。

2.谈谈你对待生活的态度。

期末综合测试题

第一部分 英语知识运用

（共分三节，满分40分）

第一节 语音知识：从 A、B、C、D 四个选项中找出其画线部分与所给单词画线部分读音相同的选项，并在答题卡上将该项涂黑。（共5分，每小题1分）

( ) 1. acc<u>o</u>mpany　　A. <u>o</u>pera　　B. c<u>o</u>nvenience　　C. <u>o</u>bject　　D. c<u>o</u>lor

( ) 2. d<u>ou</u>bt　　A. t<u>ou</u>ch　　B. sh<u>ou</u>t　　C. th<u>ou</u>gh　　D. tr<u>ou</u>ble

( ) 3. sin<u>c</u>ere　　A. <u>c</u>onnection　B. rea<u>c</u>tion　　C. <u>c</u>hance　　D. <u>c</u>ircle

( ) 4. <u>ch</u>aracter　　A. te<u>ch</u>nique　B. <u>ch</u>oice　　C. resear<u>ch</u>　D. wat<u>ch</u>er

( ) 5. h<u>ear</u>　　A. h<u>ear</u>d　　B. cl<u>ear</u>　　C. h<u>ear</u>t　　D. w<u>ear</u>

第二节 词汇与语法知识：从 A、B、C、D 四个选项中选出可以填入空白处的最佳选项，并在答题卡上将该项涂黑。（共25分，每小题1分）

( ) 6. I'm not fond of _____ music very much, but I do like _____ music they are dancing to.

　　A. the, the　　B. /, /　　C. /, the　　D. the, /

( ) 7. We can't go camping _____ the bad weather.

　　A. because　　B. because of　　C. as　　D. for

( ) 8. The correct response to a sneeze is "_____."

　　A. God bless you　B. Good luck　　C. Take care　　D. You are ill

( ) 9. We'd better not do or say something to _____ other people.

　　A. hurt　　B. wound　　C. injure　　D. destroy

( ) 10. —Will you go home this weekend?

—Yes, and _____.

A. So Li Ming will   B. Li Ming will too

C. So will Li Ming   D. So do Li Ming

( )11. _____ as China's national opera, Beijing Opera originated in the 18th century.

A. Know   B. Known   C. Knowing   D. Know

( )12. I will follow you _____ you go.

A. whenever   B. however   C. whatever   D. wherever

( )13. Only in this way _____ solve this problem.

A. we do   B. do we   C. we can   D. can we

( )14. —Would you like some beer?

—Yes, just _____.

A. little   B. a little   C. few   D. a few

( )15. Are you familiar _____ the words on the blackboard?

A. with   B. to   C. for   D. of

( )16. People sometimes feel _____ of making an apology.

A. ashaming   B. ashamed   C. shame   D. shameful

( )17. When a person apologizes to you, _____ is necessary to respond to the apology to show that you forgive the person.

A. that   B. this   C. it   D. its

( )18. Red _____ a strong feeling like anger.

A. used to express   B. is used to express

C. is used to expressing   D. used to expressing

( )19. Nowadays losing _____ is in fashion.

A. weigh   B. weight   C. weighting   D. weightless

( )20. Don't forget _____ the letter.

A. post   B. posting   C. posted   D. to post

( )21. She can't help _____ a cake because she is busy doing her homework.

A. to make   B. making   C. made   D. being made

( )22. My mother always tells me _____ out alone at night.

A. not go   B. not to go   C. go   D. don't go

( )23. Beijing Opera has nothing _____ the opera of the west.

A. in common as   B. common with

C. in common with   D. on common to

( )24. You will be ready _____ face the world of Americans _____ confidence.

　　A. to, with　　B. with, to　　C. to, to　　D. with, with

( )25. You can _____ choose an optimistic attitude _____ choose a pessimistic attitude.

　　A. neither, nor　B. both, and　C. either, or　D. not only, but also

( )26. The trousers look _____ and sell _____.

　　A. good, good　B. well, well　C. well, good　D. good, well

( )27. When someone is _____, we say that he feels blue.

　　A. with high spirits   B. in high spirits

　　C. with low spirits   D. in low spirits

( )28. Our team _____ three boy students, five girl students and two teachers.

　　A. is made of   B. is made up of

　　C. are made of   D. are made up of

( )29. I suggest _____ go at once.

　　A. she　　B. her　　C. hers　　D. herself

( )30. I prefer _____ rather than _____ a bike.

　　A. to walk, to ride   B. walking, riding

　　C. to walk, ride   D. to walk, riding

第三节　完形填空：阅读下面的短文，从所给的每组 A、B、C、D 四个选项中选择正确的答案，并在答题卡上将该项涂黑。（共 10 分，每小题 1 分）

What is your favorite __31__? Do you like yellow, orange or red? If you do, you must be an __32__ person who enjoys life. Do you like blue? Then you are probably quiet, shy and would rather follow than lead.

Colors do influence our __33__. A yellow room makes most people feel more cheerful and more relaxed than a dark green one; and a red dress brings __34__ and cheer to the saddest winter day. On __35__ hand, black is depressing. There was a black bridge over the Thames River near London. __36__ people who killed themselves on that bridge used to be larger than those on any other bridge in the area—until it __37__

green.

Light and bright colors make people not only __38__ but also more active. In the factory, the workers will work better, harder and have __39__ accidents when their machines are painted orange rather __40__ black.

( )31. A. season   B. sports   C. color   D. food
( )32. A. action   B. actor   C. act   D. active
( )33. A. moods   B. interest   C. spirit   D. hobbies
( )34. A. warm   B. warmth   C. cold   D. colder
( )35. A. the other   B. another   C. other   D. others
( )36. A. A number of   B. An amount of   C. The number of   D. The amount of
( )37. A. painted   B. was painted   C. repainted   D. was repainted
( )38. A. happy   B. happier   C. unhappy   D. unhappier
( )39. A. few   B. fewer   C. little   D. less
( )40. A. than   B. to   C. with   D. on

第二部分 篇章与词汇理解

（共分三节,满分50分）

—— ★★★ ——

第一节 阅读理解:阅读下列短文,从每题所给 A、B、C、D 四个选项中,选出最恰当的答案,并在答题卡上将该项涂黑。(共30分,每小题2分)

A

O. Henry was a pen name used by an American writer of short stories. His real name was William Sydney Porter. He was born in North Carolina in 1862. As a young boy he lived an exciting life. He did not go to school for very long, but he managed to teach himself everything he needed to know. When he was about 20 years old, O. Henry went to Texas, where he tried different jobs. He first worked on a newspaper, and then had a job in a bank. When some money went missing from the bank O. Henry was believed to have stolen it. Because of that, he was sent to prison. During the three years in prison, he learned to write short stories. After he got out of prison, he went to New York and continued writing. He wrote mostly about New York and the life of the poor there. People liked his stories, because simple as the tales were, they would finish with a sudden change at the end, to the reader's surprise.

( )41. People enjoyed reading O. Henry's stories because _____.

    A. they had surprising endings   B. they were easy to understand

    C. they showed his love for the poor   D. they were about New York City

( )42. O. Henry went to prison because _____.

    A. people thought he had stolen money from the newspaper

    B. he broke the law by not using his own name

    C. he wanted to write stories about prisoners

    D. people thought he had taken money that was not his

( )43. What do we know about O. Henry before he began writing?

    A. He was well-educated.   B. He was not serious about his work.

    C. He was devoted to the poor.   D. He was very good at learning.

( )44. Where did O. Henry get most material for his short stories?

    A. His life inside the prison.   B. The newspaper articles he wrote.

    C. The city and people of New York.   D. His exciting early life as a boy.

( )45. In which order did O. Henry do the following things?

    a. Lived in New York.   b. Worked in a bank.   c. Travelled to Texas.

    d. Was put in prison.   e. Had a newspaper Job.

    f. Learned to write stories.

    A. e. c. f. b. d. a   B. c. e. b. d. f. a

    C. e. b. d. c. a. f.   D. c. b. e. d. a. f.

B

We know the westerners like to plan for their time carefully in order to do all the things that are important to them. So if your American or English friend asks you to dinner, he usually invites you a week ahead. But if you really have no time and can't go to the dinner, you can ring him to say sorry. The dinner is usually served at home, sometimes at a restaurant. You should get there on time, and don't forget to put on your fine clothes. It is also a good idea to take some little presents to your friend, such as flowers, chocolates and so on. When you are at dinner, you should also observe (遵守) some other customs. Here I'll give you some dos and don'ts about them in the following:

Don't leave bones on the table or the floor. (You should put them on your plate with fingers.)

Don't use your bowl to drink soup, but use your spoon to help you instead.

Don't talk with much food in your mouth.

Don't ask others to have more wine. (This is quite different from that in China.)

After dinner, use your napkin(餐巾) to clean your mouth and hands.

Make sure small pieces of food are not left on your face.

Then after dinner, you can stay there a little time. And your friend will be pleased if you leave in half an hour or so. Next day, you had better ring him up to thank him for the good dinner.

(　　)46. If your American or English friend wants to invite you to dinner, he will invite you _____.

  A. a week before the dinner　　B. on the day before the dinner

  C. on the night before the dinner　　D. at the last moment

(　　)47. When you go to your friend's for dinner, _____.

  A. you can go there whenever you like

  B. you can put on your common clothes

  C. you'd better take a little present

  D. you can take another friend if you want to do so

(　　)48. It would be polite to _____.

  A. put bones on your plates with fingers

  B. persuade others to drink more

  C. drink soup with your bowl

  D. talk with much food in your mouth

(　　)49. Which of the following is true?

  A. After dinner, you'd better stay and talk with your friends for a long time to show your thanks.

  B. You needn't ring your friend the next day to show your thanks.

  C. After dinner, you'd better leave in half an hour.

  D. After dinner, use your hand to clean your mouth.

(　　)50. The passage mainly tells us _____.

  A. when your friend asks you to dinner

  B. what should you do if you have dinner with your friend

C. take a little present for your friend

D. the customs you should observe when you are at dinner

C

Have you ever wondered why birds sing? Maybe you thought that they were just happy. After all, you probably sing when you are happy.

Some scientists believe that birds do sing some of the time just because they are happy. However, they sing most of the time for a very different reason. Their singing is actually a warning to other birds to stay out of their territory.

Do you know what a "territory" is? A territory is an area that an animal, usually the male, claims(声称) as its own. Only he and his family are welcome there. No other families of the same species are welcome. Your house is your territory where only your family and friends are welcome. If a stranger should enter your territory and threaten you, you might shout. Probably this would be enough to frighten him away.

If so, you have actually frightened the stranger away without having to fight him. A bird does the same thing. But he expects an outsider almost any time, especially at nesting(筑巢) season. So he is screaming all the time, whether he can see an outsider or not. This <u>screaming</u> is what we call a bird's song, and it is usually enough to keep an outsider away.

( )51. Some scientists believe that most of the time bird's singing is actually _____.

    A. a way of warning   B. an expression of happiness

    C. a way of greeting   D. an expression of anger

( )52. What is a bird's "territory"?

    A. A place where families of other species are not accepted.

    B. A place where a bird may shout at the top of its voice.

    C. An area for which birds fight against each other.

    D. An area which a bird considers to be its own.

( )53. Why do birds keep on singing at nesting season?

    A. Because they want to invite more friends.

    B. Because they want to find outsiders around.

    C. Because their singing helps frighten outsiders away.

    D. Because their singing helps get rid of their fears.

( )54. How does the writer explain birds' singing?

 A. By comparing birds with human beings.

 B. By reporting experiment results.

 C. By describing birds' daily life.

 D. By telling a bird's story.

( )55. What does the underlined word "screaming" in paragraph 4 mean?

 A. 哭喊声. B. 令人惊愕的. C. 尖叫的. D. 尖叫声.

第二节　词义搭配:从(B)栏中选出(A)栏单词的正确解释,并在答题卡上将该项涂黑。(共10分,每小题1分)

(A)	(B)
(　)56. Red Cross	A. go with
(　)57. occasion	B. say sorry to sb.
(　)58. admit	C. go on doing
(　)59. apologize	D. an international organization
(　)60. continue	E. say falsely
(　)61. accompany	F. astonishing
(　)62. pretend	G. agree to the truth of usually something bad
(　)63. set up	H. make or become stronger
(　)64. amazing	I. opportunity, particular time
(　)65. strengthen	J. build, found

第三节　补全对话:根据对话内容,从对话后的选项中选出能填入空白处的最佳选项,并在答题卡上将该项涂黑。(共10分,每小题2分)

A: Hi, Carol! ___66___

B: Oh, hi, Darren. I am just getting ready for the Red Nose Day concert tomorrow.

A: Really? Well, I'm free this afternoon. ___67___

A: In fact, I have really finished. Jim and I are going to put up some ads later. Could you please help us with that?

A: ___68___

B: That's wonderful! Oh, there is one more thing. Would you mind coming to help sell tickets at the door early tomorrow?

A: Not at all. __69__

B: Around six would be great.

A: OK. __70__

B: See you.

> A. No problem.
> B. See you then.
> C. Of course not.
> D. What are you doing?
> E. Can I give you a hand?
> F. What time shall I be there?
> G. Have you finished your homework?

第三部分　语言技能运用

（共分四节,满分30分）

——★★★——

第一节　单词拼写：根据下列句子及所给汉语注释,在答题卡上相应题号后的横线上写出该单词。(共5分,每小题1分)

71. Life is all about _____ (选择).

72. It is quite _____ (粗鲁的) to speak to others with your mouth full.

73. When we can't make a _____ (决定), we frown.

74. The _____ (形状) of a heart is used to mean love.

75. Don't lose your _____ (脾气) with other people.

第二节　词形变换：用括号内单词的适当形式填空,将正确答案写在答题卡上相应题号后的横线上。(共5分,每小题1分)

76. _____ (General) speaking, young people like pop music.

77. Chous are basically the clowns _____ (mark) by a small square-shaped white color on their noses.

78. I hope that you can answer my questions _____ (honest).

79. Ma Yun is very _____ (success) in his business.

80. Over 150 years after their creation, blue jeans in _____ (vary) styles are

still very much in fashion.

第三节 改错:从 A、B、C、D 四个画线处找出一处错误的选项填入答题卡上相应题号后的括号内,并在横线上写出正确答案。(共 10 分,每小题 2 分)

81. My sister <u>prefers</u> <u>staying</u> home alone <u>than</u> <u>going</u> shopping with me.
               A   B   C   D

82. He <u>explained</u> where he <u>went</u> yesterday <u>for</u> me <u>carefully</u>.
           A   B   C   D

83. <u>This</u> is <u>known</u> to all <u>that</u> the moon <u>runs</u> around the sun.
   A   B   C   D

84. <u>Only</u> when we <u>grow up</u> <u>we can</u> realize <u>how much</u> our parents love us.
   A   B   C   D

85. <u>Although</u> the work <u>is very</u> difficult, <u>but</u> I have finished it <u>by myself</u>.
     A   B   C   D

81. (　　)应为_____　　　　82. (　　)应为_____

83. (　　)应为_____　　　　84. (　　)应为_____

85. (　　)应为_____

第四节 书面表达。(共 10 分)

作文题目:The Mobile Phones at School。

词数要求:80~100 词。

写作要点:1. 越来越多的学生开始带手机进校园,手机已经成为中学校园里的一个问题。

2. 手机带入校园的弊端。

3. 呼吁禁止带手机入校园。

综合模拟试题(一)

第一部分 英语知识运用

（共分三节，满分40分）

——★★★——

第一节 语音知识：从 A、B、C、D 四个选项中找出其画线部分与所给单词画线部分读音相同的选项，并在答题卡上将该项涂黑。（共5分，每小题1分）

( ) 1. br<u>ea</u>th　　A. gr<u>ea</u>t　　B. br<u>ea</u>the　　C. br<u>ea</u>d　　D. rep<u>ea</u>t

( ) 2. walk<u>ed</u>　　A. help<u>ed</u>　　B. play<u>ed</u>　　C. divid<u>ed</u>　　D. manag<u>ed</u>

( ) 3. h<u>ea</u>lthy　　A. <u>y</u>es　　B. honest<u>y</u>　　C. rel<u>y</u>　　D. gu<u>y</u>

( ) 4. attit<u>u</u>de　　A. s<u>u</u>gar　　B. f<u>u</u>ture　　C. s<u>u</u>mmer　　D. h<u>u</u>rry

( ) 5. w<u>ar</u>m　　A. sm<u>ar</u>t　　B. p<u>ar</u>t　　C. l<u>ar</u>ge　　D. qu<u>ar</u>ter

第二节 词汇与语法知识：从 A、B、C、D 四个选项中选出可以填入空白处的最佳选项，并在答题卡上将该项涂黑。（共25分，每小题1分）

( ) 6. The young boy has turned _____ writer.
　　A. a　　B. /　　C. the　　D. an

( ) 7. The resort is about _____ the Summer Palace.
　　A. twice the size of　　　　B. two times as the size of
　　C. as twice big as　　　　　D. two times bigger as

( ) 8. We must do all we can _____ all the children can be taken good care of.
　　A. make sure　　B. be sure of　　C. to make sure　　D. to be sure of

( ) 9. He must _____ abroad, I haven't seen him for a long time.
　　A. go　　B. went　　C. have gone　　D. go to

93

( )10. —How many students are in the classroom now?

—_____.

A. No one   B. Nobody   C. None   D. Not one

( )11. John needs our help, _____ he?

A. need   B. needn't   C. does   D. doesn't

( )12. This is _____ news that all of us are excited at it.

A. so good   B. such good   C. so a good   D. such a good

( )13. She finished the work by herself, _____ made us very surprised.

A. that   B. what   C. which   D. it

( )14. _____ good weather we are having these days.

A. What a   B. How a   C. What   D. How

( )15. His first book was published in his _____.

A. thirty   B. thirtyth   C. thirty's   D. thirties

( )16. —Did you know Mr. Li?

—Certainly, I _____ him before he worked in our company.

A. had known   B. knew   C. have known   D. know

( )17. The weather is hotter and hotter, but soon you will be used to _____ outdoors.

A. work   B. working   C. worked   D. being worked

( )18. Neither the girl nor the couple _____ him very well.

A. knows   B. knowing   C. know   D. are knowing

( )19. Many adults _____ mobile phones now.

A. addict to   B. addict with   C. are addicted to   D. are addicted with

( ) 20. Most bosses insisted that every minute _____ made full use of _____ the work well.

A. be;doing   B. be;to do   C. was;doing   D. was;to do

( )21. When you are in need, you can _____ others for help.

A. turn on   B. turn off   C. turn to   D. turn

( )22. China lies _____ the west of Japan.

A. in   B. on   C. at   D. to

( )23. I found _____ was difficult to understand.

A. which my teacher said   B. that my teacher said

    C. what my teacher said   D. when my teacher said

( )24. Many people couldn't help _____ at the happy news.

    A. laugh   B. laughing   C. to laugh   D. laughed

( )25. When I got to the airport, the plane had _____.

    A. taken off   B. took off   C. taken away   D. took away

( )26. It was Tom _____ didn't finish the homework.

    A. which   B. whom   C. for whom   D. who

( )27. It is the first time you _____ such a mistake.

    A. made   B. will make   C. have made   D. had made

( )28. I don't think he can finish the work alone, _____?

    A. do I   B. don't I   C. can he   D. can't he

( )29. Who is _____ boy in your class?

    A. the tall   B. the taller   C. the tallest   D. tallest

( )30. —Who did you go to Beijing with?

    —_____.

    A. Smiths   B. the Smiths   C. Smiths'   D. the Smiths'

第三节 完形填空:阅读下面的短文,从所给的每组 **A、B、C、D** 四个选项中选择正确的答案,并在答题卡上将该项涂黑。(共 10 分,每小题 1 分)

  It was the afternoon of April 1. The bell rang __31__ the end of school. The students __32__ their books into their bags. They were ready __33__ home.

  Just at the moment, their English teacher came into the classroom and said to them, "Hello, boys and girls. Now go over the English lessons, and we'll have a test __34__ half an hour." __35__ these words, she left.

  The students looked at each other in surprise. How sudden! The teacher had never told them they would have a test, yet they took out their English books and began to work hard.

  They studied and studied. It was getting dark, __36__ the teacher hadn't come yet!

  The monitor went out to the teachers' office. __37__ minutes later, the English teacher came in with a smile. But she had __38__ in her hand!

  "I'm sorry, but do you know __39__?" she said.

  After the students heard this, they couldn't help __40__ and saying "April Fools!"

( )31. A. on B. in C. for D. at

( )32. A. put B. were put C. would put D. were putting

( )33. A. to go B. go C. going D. went

( )34. A. in B. after C. later D. out

( )35. A. Without B. With C. For D. In

( )36. A. and B. but C. or D. so

( )37. A. Few B. Little C. A few D. A little

( )38. A. something B. nothing C. everything D. anything

( )39. A. what day is today B. what's the date
　　　C. what day today is D. what the date is

( )40. A. laugh B. to laugh C. laughed D. laughing

第二部分　篇章与词汇理解

（共分三节，满分 50 分）

第一节　阅读理解：阅读下列短文，从每题所给 A、B、C、D 四个选项中，选出最恰当的答案，并在答题卡上将该项涂黑。（共 30 分，每小题 2 分）

A

People used to say,"The hand that rocks（摇）the cradle（摇篮）rules the world" and "Behind every successful man there is a woman."

Both these sayings mean the same thing. Men rule the world, but their mothers and wives rule them.

Most American women wish to make their husbands and sons successful, but some of them want more for themselves. They want good jobs. When they work they want to be better paid. They want to be as successful as men.

The American women's liberation movement was started by women who didn't want to stand behind successful men. They wanted to stand beside men, with the same chance for success. They refused to work side by side with men who do the same work for a higher pay.

A liberated woman must be proud of being a woman and have confidence（自信）in herself. If somebody says to her "You have come a long way, baby," she will smile and answer,"Not nearly as far as I'm going to go,baby!"

This movement is quite new,and many American women don't agree yet. But it has already made some important changes in women's lives— in men's lives,too.

(   )41. "Behind every successful man there is a woman" means _____.

　　A. men are always successful but not women

　　B. women are not willing to stand in front of men

　　C. women do play an important part in men's lives and work

　　D. women can be as successful as men

(   )42. Which of the following is NOT true?

　　A. Some American women want to work side by side with men and get the same pay for the same work.

　　B. Most American women want to be more successful than men.

　　C. Not every American woman wants to get a job.

　　D. The American women's liberation movement did make some changes in women's lives.

(   )43. According to the passage,many American women today are _____.

　　A. still going a long way to work

　　B. working at easier jobs than men

　　C. unwilling to work side by side with men

　　D. willing to be less important than men as they used to

(   )44. "Not nearly as far as I'm going to go" means _____.

　　A. I'm still going to work farther away from home

　　B. I'm not going to work far away from home

　　C. I'm not satisfied with what I've done

　　D. What I have done is not far from success

(   )45. The American women's liberation movement _____.

　　A. has still a long way to go

　　B. is a failure

　　C. was started by many successful women

　　D. is a new thing not accepted by the writer

B

One day an ant was drinking at a small stream and fell in. She made desperate efforts to reach the side, but made no progress at all. The poor ant almost exhausted but was still bravely doing her best when a dove(鸽子) saw her. Moved with pity, the bird threw her a blade of grass, which supported her like a raft(竹筏), and thus the ant reached the bank again. While she was resting and drying herself in the grass, she heard a man come near. He was walking along barefooted with a gun in his hand. As soon as he saw the dove, he wished to kill it. He would certainly have done so, but the ant bit him in the foot just as he raised his gun to fire. He stopped to see what had bit him, and the dove immediately flew away. It was an animal much weaker and smaller than herself that had saved her life.

( )46. The ant could not reach the side though _____.

A. she cried for help B. she asked the dove to save her

C. she tried very hard D. she could smell well

( )47. The dove saved the ant because _____.

A. she was the ant's friend

B. she took pity on the poor ant

C. the ant was almost exhausted

D. the ant had been struggled in the water for a long time

( )48. The ant succeeded in getting on the bank with the help of _____.

A. a leaf B. a piece of wood

C. a blade of grass D. a raft

( )49. Just as the man shot at the dove, _____.

A. the dove immediately flew away

B. the dove hid himself in the grass

C. the ant told the dove to leave at once

D. he felt something biting him in the foot

( )50. In writing the story, the writer wants to show _____.

A. how clever the ant was

B. how kind the dove was

C. how the ant and the dove helped each other

D. we often need help from others, therefore we should help others as much as we can

C

In recent years, advances in medical technology have made it possible for people to live longer than in the past. New medicines and machines are being developed every day to extend life. However, some people, including some doctors, are not in favor of these life-extending measures, and they argue that people should have the right to die when they want. They say that the quality of life is as important as life itself, and that people should not be forced to go on living when conditions of life have become unbearable(不可忍耐的). They say that people should be allowed to die with dignity and to decide when they want to die. Others argue that life under any conditions is better than death and that the duty of doctors is always to extend life as long as possible. And so the battle goes on and on without a definite answer.

( )51. In recent years, people can live longer than in the past. It is because of _____.

    A. the development of new medicines and machines

    B. good medical workers

    C. well-equipped big hospitals

    D. new medicines and good conditions

( )52. Some people insist that whether a dying patient has the right to die or not is up to _____.

    A. the surroundings   B. his other family members

    C. the patient himself   D. the doctors

( ) 53. From the passage we can learn that some people, including some doctors, think that _____.

    A. neither death nor life is good   B. life is better than death

    C. death is better than life   D. None of the above

( )54. Which of the following is right?

    A. The argument has ended in favor of the doctor.

    B. Most of the medical workers join in the argument.

    C. People shouldn't be allowed to die because of dignity.

    D. The argument has not ended yet.

( )55. The best title for this passage is _____.

    A. The Right to Die   B. The Right to Live

    C. Death or Life   D. The Doctor's Duty

第二节 词义搭配:从(B)栏中选出(A)栏单词的正确解释,并在答题卡上将该项涂黑。(共10分,每小题1分)

(A)	(B)
(　)56. dangerous	A. make or become stronger
(　)57. patient	B. to restrict to be a number or amount
(　)58. limit	C. not telling lies
(　)59. injure	D. not safe
(　)60. tireless	E. person who is receiving a medical treatment
(　)61. strengthen	F. make dirty
(　)62. honest	G. hurt
(　)63. private	H. never feel tired
(　)64. pollute	I. say sorry to somebody
(　)65. apologize	J. of one person, secret

第三节 补全对话:根据对话内容,从对话后的选项中选出能填入空白处的最佳选项,并在答题卡上将该项涂黑。(共10分,每小题2分)

(*Peter likes to show off. He is now talking to Lily about his new car.*)

P: I'm so excited.　66　

L: That's nice.

P: Want to go for a ride? It's a beautiful day outside.

L:　67　

P: What? You must be crazy!

L: You always think you're that great.

P: Excuse me.　68　

L: Don't you think you're showing off?

P: Well,　69　

L: You see, that's what I mean.

P: Is someone turning a little green here?

L:　70　Nobody admire you just because you are rich.

A. No, thanks.

B. What do you mean?

C. I can't believe my parents got me a new car for my birthday!

D. but it's really a wonderful car.

E. No, never.

第三部分　语言技能运用

（共分四节,满分 30 分）

——★★★——

第一节　单词拼写:根据下列句子及所给汉语注释,在答题卡上相应题号后的横线上写出该单词。（共 5 分,每小题 1 分）

71. We should do everything with _____（信心）.

72. Before finding a job, you'd better prepare a(an) _____（申请书）.

73. Every situation is a _____（选择）.

74. Ads could sometimes _____（误导） consumers.

75. When he was a child, he could _____（养活） himself.

第二节　词形变换:用括号内单词的适当形式填空,将正确答案写在答题卡上相应题号后的横线上。（共 5 分,每小题 1 分）

76. The total _____ (long) of the road is over 5,000km.

77. Even the beautiful birds _____ (fly) in the sky are dressed in black and gray.

78. _____ (luck), he was badly injured in the earthquake.

79. Red is used to express a strong _____ (feel) like anger.

80. They don't come from France, they are _____ (German).

第三节　改错:从 A、B、C、D 四个画线处找出一处错误的选项填入答题卡上相应题号后的括号内,并在横线上写出正确答案。（共 10 分,每小题 2 分）

81. How noise they are making.
　　A　　B　　C　　　D

82. Having told many times, he still couldn't understand it.
　　　A　　　　　B　　　　　C　　　D

83. We should try our best to solve the problem, whatever difficult it is.
          A   B   C   D

84. He made a great progress by working hard.
       A   B   C   D

85. I felt like to cry when I failed my English test.
       A   B   C   D

81. (　　)应为_____　　　　82. (　　)应为_____

83. (　　)应为_____　　　　84. (　　)应为_____

85. (　　)应为_____

第四节　书面表达。(共10分)

作文题目:Our Life in the Future。

词数要求:80~100 词。

写作要点:1. 未来交通便利。

　　　　2. 教育方式多样化,医学更发达。

　　　　3. 集娱乐与购物为一体的网上购物中心使生活更精彩。

综合模拟试题(二)

第一部分 英语知识运用

（共分三节，满分40分）

第一节 语音知识：从 A、B、C、D 四个选项中找出其画线部分与所给单词画线部分读音相同的选项，并在答题卡上将该项涂黑。（共5分，每小题1分）

( )1. s<u>ea</u>son A. w<u>ea</u>ther B. m<u>ea</u>n C. r<u>ea</u>dy D. d<u>ea</u>th

( )2. c<u>u</u>rrent A. b<u>u</u>siness B. s<u>u</u>ccess C. p<u>u</u>ll D. <u>a</u>dult

( )3. brea<u>th</u> A. <u>th</u>ough B. clo<u>th</u>es C. grow<u>th</u> D. <u>th</u>us

( )4. relax<u>ed</u> A. earn<u>ed</u> B. afford<u>ed</u>
              C. plead<u>ed</u> D. develop<u>ed</u>

( )5. s<u>i</u>ght A. s<u>y</u>mbol B. bes<u>i</u>des C. mus<u>i</u>c D. As<u>i</u>an

第二节 词汇与语法知识：从 A、B、C、D 四个选项中选出可以填入空白处的最佳选项，并在答题卡上将该项涂黑。（共25分，每小题1分）

( ) 6. The warmth of _____ sweater which my mother bought me can protect me from any cold in winter.
   A. a   B. an   C. the   D. /

( )7. He gave me _____ useful information that I finished the task in time.
   A. such   B. such a   C. so   D. so a

( )8. China has a larger population than _____ country in the world.
   A. other   B. any other   C. any one   D. others

( )9. He succeeded _____.
   A. in his fifty   B. in his fifties   C. in the fifty   D. in the fifties

( )10. He is _____ to lift the heavy box.

　　A. too strong　　B. so strong　　C. strong enough　D. enough strong

( )11. Listen! The family must be quarreling, _____?

　　A. mustn't it　　B. mustn't they　　C. isn't it　　D. aren't they

( )12. _____ alone in the dark street, I felt so frightened as to cry.

　　A. Walking　　B. Having walked　C. Walked　　D. Being walked

( )13. Could you tell me _____ in the English Alphabet?

　　A. how many letters there are　　B. how many letters are there

　　C. how many letters are　　D. how many there are letters

( )14. Not only I but also Jane and Mary _____ tired after having one exam after another.

　　A. am　　B. is　　C. are　　D. be

( )15. Never _____ heard my mother sing before.

　　A. I have　　B. have I　　C. I had　　D. had I

( )16. It is important _____ you _____ out for some fresh breath.

　　A. of; to go　　B. of; going　　C. for; to go　　D. for; going

( )17. Staying in a hotel for a day is _____ renting a room for a week.

　　A. twice as much as　　B. as much as twice

　　C. as twice as much　　D. twice than

( )18. We are not allowed _____ the lab without the permission of our teacher.

　　A. to enter　　B. entering　　C. entered　　D. enter

( )19. The house wants _____ after such a long time.

　　A. to paint　　B. to be painted　　C. being painted　D. to be paint

( )20. The girl was named Florence _____ her birthplace.

　　A. with　　B. for　　C. about　　D. after

( )21. I have never heard the news _____ he graduated from a famous university.

　　A. which　　B. that　　C. who　　D. whom

( )22. _____ you, I wouldn't have said such words to my loved one.

　　A. Were I　　B. If I were　　C. If I had　　D. Had I been

( )23. We'd better not go fishing tomorrow if it _____.

  A. rains   B. will rain   C. rained   D. is raining

( )24. He pretended _____ when I passed his desk.
  A. to read   B. to be reading   C. reading   D. being read

( )25. Can you remember the park where we _____ in summer?
  A. used to swim   B. used to swimming
  C. are used to swimming   D. are used to swim

( )26. May you _____ in your driving test?
  A. success   B. succeed   C. succeeded   D. successful

( )27. It won't be long _____ smoking is not allowed in public areas.
  A. before   B. after   C. since   D. for

( )28. The woman _____ to dinner yesterday is a friend of my mother's.
  A. coming   B. to come   C. came   D. being come

( )29. Alice watched carefully _____ she could discover what she needed.
  A. in order to   B. so as to   C. in order that   D. in such that

( )30. _____ you have known the rules, let's begin!
  A. Because   B. Now that   C. For   D. Because of

第三节　完形填空：阅读下面的短文，从所给的每组 A、B、C、D 四个选项中选择正确的答案，并在答题卡上将该项涂黑。（共 10 分，每小题 1 分）

  A new study has __31__ no evidence that sunscreen(防晒剂), __32__ to reduce the risk of skin cancer, in fact increases the risk.

  Researchers from the University of Iowa based their findings on a review of 18 earlier studies that looked at the association between sunscreen use and melanoma(黑素瘤). They said __33__ they found flaws in studies that had reported associations between sunscreen use and higher risk of melanoma.

  Most health experts believe that by protecting the skin __34__ the harmful __35__ of the sun, sunscreen helps to prevent skin cancer, __36__ is increasing in incidence(发生率) faster than __37__ cancer in the United States.

  But questions have been raised about sunscreen and whether it may have opposite effect, perhaps by allowing people __38__ exposed to the sun longer without __39__.

  The researchers said that among the problems with some earlier studies is that they often failed to take into account that those people are more likely to use sunscreen.

As __40__ result, it may appear that sunscreen users get cancer more often.

( )31. A. find B. found C. founded D. finding
( )32. A. use B. used C. using D. to use
( )33. A. what B. who C. which D. that
( )34. A. from B. to C. with D. in
( )35. A. affects B. affacts C. effects D. effacts
( )36. A. that B. which C. who D. whose
( )37. A. other B. the other C. another D. any other
( )38. A. remain B. remaining C. remained D. to remain
( )39. A. burn B. burning C. burned D. to burn
( )40. A. a B. an C. the D. /

第二部分 篇章与词汇理解

(共分三节,满分50分)

——★★★——

第一节 阅读理解:阅读下列短文,从每题所给A、B、C、D四个选项中,选出最恰当的答案,并在答题卡上将该项涂黑。(共30分,每小题2分)

A

In the United States 84 colleges now accept just women. Most of them were established in the 19th century; they were designed to offer women the education they couldn't receive anywhere else. At that time major universities and colleges accepted only men. In the past 20 years many young women have chosen to study at colleges that accept both men and women. As a result, some women's colleges decided to accept men students, too. Others, however, refused to change. Now these schools are popular again.

The headmaster of Trinity College in Washington D.C. said that by the end of the 1980s women began to recognize that studying at the same school with men did not mean women were having an equal chance to learn. The headmaster of Smith College in Massachusetts says a women's college permits women to choose classes and activities freely. For example she says that in a women's college a higher percentage of students study mathematics than in a college with both men and women.

Educational experts say men students in the United States usually speak in class more than women students do. In a women's college, women feel free to say what they think. Women's schools also bring out leadership abilities in many women. Women are represented(作为示范) everywhere. For example, at a women's college, every governing office is held by a woman. Recent studies show this leadership continues after college. The studies show that American women who went to women's colleges are more likely to hold successful jobs later in life.

(   )41. Most of women's colleges were established _____.

    A. to give women the education they could not receive anywhere else

    B. to separate women from men

    C. to offer women special chances for work

    D. to help women have more study opportunities

(   )42. Some women's colleges decided to accept men students because _____.

    A. teaching women is more difficult than teaching men

    B. many young women chose to study at colleges with both men and women

    C. studying with men is more challenging

    D. women and men can have equal chances of competition

(   )43. From the passage we know that _____.

    A. more and more women's colleges are being established now

    B. more and more women like to study in colleges with both men and women

    C. there are more women's colleges than colleges with both men and women in the USA

    D. both Trinity College and Smith College are women's colleges

(   )44. According to the passage, if a woman wants to hold successful jobs, she'd better _____.

    A. study in colleges with both men and women

    B. study in Trinity College

    C. learn from the headmaster of Smith College

    D. study in women's colleges

(   )45. The best title for the passage is _____.

    A. Types of American Colleges   B. American Women's Colleges

    C. Education in America   D. The Difference Between Men and Women

B

The ideal(理想的) teacher may be young or old, tall or short, fat or thin. He should know his subject, but he can make mistakes if he is unwilling to learn. His personality is as important as his knowledge. The ideal teacher should be warm-hearted. He must never teach anything he is not interested in. He should be a bit of an actor and he should not be afraid to show his feelings and express his likes and dislikes. He must like his students and respect them. But he must also respect himself and be proud of his work. Otherwise, he cannot respect his students and win respect from them. The ideal teacher should have an understanding of his students and be able to relate to them. He needs students' understanding, too. The ideal teacher should be kind, encouraging and helpful and he should encourage his students to seek knowledge. The ideal teacher should see his students as individuals and admit their differences. He must know how to encourage the self-development and growth of each of his students. The ideal teacher is one who grows, learns and improves himself along with his students.

So what about the teachers around you?

(　　)46. Which of the following is the least important in judging an ideal teacher according to the passage?

　　A. His age and looks.　　　　B. His personality.

　　C. His knowledge.　　　　　　D. His attitude towards his students.

(　　)47. Can an ideal teacher make mistakes?

　　A. No. He should be very careful and not to make any mistakes.

　　B. Yes. Because no one can be perfect.

　　C. No. He should always be the authority to his students.

　　D. Yes. But he should be willing to learn.

(　　)48. What relationship should be built between an ideal teacher and his students according to the passage?

　　A. Mutual respect and understanding.

　　B. Mutual encouragement and help.

　　C. Mutual aid and affection.

　　D. Mutual support and inspiration.

(　　)49. How does an ideal teacher view(看待) his students?

　　A. He views them as talented young people.

B. He views them as different from each other.

C. He views them as self-centered(自我的)individuals.

D. He views them as understanding, respectful individuals.

( )50. Which of the following can be inferred from the passage?

A. An ideal teacher should always set an example for his students.

B. Teachers and students benefit from each other in the process of teaching and learning.

C. Students should never expect their teachers to be ideal.

D. Those who are trying to improve themselves constantly are ideal teachers.

C

For years, many people would not believe that smoke could attack so many parts of the body in so many ways. Study shows, however, that tobacco isn't one single thing. At least 60% of it is gas—20 different kinds of gases. And one of these is the deadly carbon monoxide (CO).

In factories, the amount of this gas in the air is measured and it must be kept under fixed safe level. But there is 640 times this safe amount in cigarette smoke.

Oxygen is carried through your body by the red blood cells(细胞). But this poison gas, CO, will get to the blood cells before the oxygen can. So, if you smoke your blood carries five to ten times more of this deadly gas than normal. To make up for this, your body must make more red cells.

The oxygen in your blood passes into your tissue(组织). But here again CO makes trouble. It keeps the oxygen from passing into your tissue as fast as it should. Because of this cigarette country is always about 8,000 feet above sea level. Someone who smokes and lives at sea level gets as little oxygen as a nonsmoker at a height of nearly two miles. This happens to everyone who smokes, no matter how old or how young. Anyone who completes in sports can tell you that those who smoke run out of breath more quickly than those who don't.

( )51. The gas amount in cigarette smoke is _____.

A. 640 times higher than the gas safe levels in factories

B. 640 times lower than the gas safe levels in factories

C. 640 times as much as that in factories

D. as dangerous as that in factories

( )52. If you smoke, _____.

A. Your blood carries more oxygen than normal

B. your blood carries much more CO than normal

C. you can have five to ten times of blood than usual

D. your blood will be poisonous

( )53. Those who smoke _____.

A. all live at sea level

B. don't live at a height of two miles

C. breathe as much oxygen as nonsmokers

D. only get the same amount of oxygen at the sea level as nonsmokers at a height of two miles

( )54. Smokers are _____.

A. easily hurt   B. easily excited   C. easily tired   D. healthy

( )55. Which statement is NOT true according to the passage?

A. Many people believed that smoke couldn't attack so many parts of the body in so many ways for years.

B. The carbon monoxide will get to the blood cells before the oxygen.

C. If you smoke, your blood carries five to ten times more of oxygen than normal.

D. A runner who smokes runs out of breath more quickly than the one who doesn't smoke.

第二节　词义搭配：从(B)栏中选出(A)栏单词的正确解释，并在答题卡上将该项涂黑。(共10分，每小题1分)

(A)　　　　　　　　　　　　(B)

( )56. occur   A. an expression of not satisfaction

( )57. establish   B. to happen or take place

( )58. private   C. worth a lot of money

( )59. complaint   D. only one, not more

( )60. disease   E. to be full of life and energy

( )61. single   F. to set up or found

( )62. lively   G. belonging to the body

( )63. fail   H. personal, in person

( )64. valuable   I. not to be successful

( )65. physical   J. illness

第三节 补全对话:根据对话内容,从对话后的选项中选出能填入空白处的最佳选项,并在答题卡上将该项涂黑。(共10分,每小题2分)

M: Help yourself to some chocolates. Chen Li brought them from Shanghai.

C: __66__ I can't eat anything sweet. It's my teeth.

M: I'm sorry to hear that. __67__?

C: I did. He told me that I have to have one tooth out and two filled. But I can't find time for it.

M: __68__.

C: But I'm busy now. I think I'll go next week.

M: I'm afraid you'd better go right now. The sooner you do something about it, the better.

C: __69__ Can you please tell our head that I'll be back by lunchtime?

M: __70__.

C: Thank you very much. See you this afternoon.

M: See you.

A. If I were you, I'd take care of them right away.
B. You'd better not worry about yourself.
C. I agree with you.
D. Thanks.
E. With pleasure.
F. Did you see a dentist?
G. Here you are.

第三部分 语言技能运用

（共分四节，满分 30 分）

———★★★———

第一节 单词拼写：根据下列句子及所给汉语注释,在答题卡上相应题号后的横线上写出该单词。（共 5 分,每小题 1 分）

71. The author had all his works _____ （出版）before he died.

72. A _____ （自私的）behavior will cause great damage to others.

73. He accepted the _____ （具有挑战性的）work and did it very well.

74. Dumplings are _____ （传统的）food during the Spring Festival.

75. Girls are good at making flowers with _____ （彩色的）paper.

第二节 词形变换：用括号内单词的适当形式填空,将正确答案写在答题卡上相应题号后的横线上。（共 5 分,每小题 1 分）

76. Reading English novels is of great _____ (important) in learning English.

77. We can express our feelings with words or _____ (face) expressions.

78. We should make an _____ (apologize) when we do something wrong.

79. _____ (luck), he failed in the entrance examination.

80. The zoo needs better _____ (manage) rather than more money.

第三节 改错：从 A、B、C、D 四个画线处找出一处错误的选项填入答题卡上相应题号后的括号内,并在横线上写出正确答案。（共 10 分,每小题 2 分）

81. The school that Bill once studied has become famous.
　　　　　A　　　B　　　　C　　　　D

82. The grass can grow as taller as 20 feet in a month.
　　　　A　　　B　　　　C　D

83. It is during the summer when we went to the Olympic park.
　　A　　B　　　　　C　　　D

84. My father suddenly returned home from America at a rainy night.
　　　　　A　　　　B　　　　　　　　　C　D

85. That is interesting for everyone to travel around the world.
　A　　B　　　C　　　D

81.（　）应为_____　　　　82.（　）应为_____

83.（　）应为_____　　　　84.（　）应为_____

85.（　）应为_____

第四节 书面表达。(共 10 分)

作文题目:The Advantages and Disadvantages of Studying Abroad。

词数要求:80~100 词。

写作要点:1.结合自己的观点阐述出国学习的利弊。

   2.参考词汇:advanced,spread,negative aspect,further education。

综合模拟试题(三)

第一部分　英语知识运用

（共分三节，满分 40 分）

——★★★——

第一节　语音知识：从 A、B、C、D 四个选项中找出其画线部分与所给单词画线部分读音相同的选项，并在答题卡上将该项涂黑。（共 5 分，每小题 1 分）

(　　)1. silent　　　A. online　　　B. selfish　　　C. movie　　　D. spirit

(　　)2. send　　　A. honest　　　B. hotel　　　C. result　　　D. perfect

(　　)3. sorrow　　A. worry　　　B. smoke　　　C. lemon　　　D. college

(　　)4. blood　　　A. cook　　　B. football　　C. flood　　　D. tooth

(　　)5. eager　　　A. design　　　B. signal　　　C. manage　　　D. change

第二节　词汇与语法知识：从 A、B、C、D 四个选项中选出可以填入空白处的最佳选项，并在答题卡上将该项涂黑。（共 25 分，每小题 1 分）

(　　)6. There is _____ M on _____ T-shirt Mary wears.
　　A. the, a　　B. a, the　　C. an, the　　D. the, the

(　　)7. —Have you finished the papers related to the children?
　　—No, please give me _____.
　　A. five another minutes　　　B. five more minute
　　C. another five minutes　　　D. more five minute

(　　)8. I apologized _____ you _____ being late again.
　　A. for, to　　B. to, for　　C. with, for　　D. for, with

(　　)9. —I have never seen such an interesting film before.
　　—_____.

A. So have I　　B. So I have　　C. Nor have I　　D. Nor I have

(　　)10. She didn't know _____ he had been given.

　　A. how many information　　　　B. how many informations

　　C. how much information　　　　D. how much informations

(　　)11. He insisted that the boy _____ to hospital at once.

　　A. send　　B. sent　　C. be sent　　D. sending

(　　)12. Don't leave the water _____ when you brush your teeth.

　　A. run　　B. runs　　C. runing　　D. running

(　　)13. He has two sons, both of _____ are doctors.

　　A. that　　B. which　　C. whom　　D. who

(　　)14. It is because of the heavy rain _____ we put off the sports meeting.

　　A. what　　B. who　　C. that　　D. when

(　　)15. Out _____ of the room angrily and cried sadly.

　　A. he rushed　　B. rushed he　　C. he rushes　　D. rushes he

(　　)16. I had trouble _____ what he said.

　　A. understand　　B. understood　　C. understanding　　D. to understand

(　　)17. He came in with a _____ cigarette between his two fingers.

　　A. light　　B. lit　　C. lighting　　D. lighted

(　　)18. Her mother has been ill _____ she came to America last year.

　　A. since　　B. for　　C. as　　D. when

(　　)19. It is high time that we _____ our environment for our children.

　　A. protect　　B. protected　　C. protecting　　D. to protect

(　　)20. —How many kangaroos did you see in the Wild Animal Park yesterday?

　　—_____.

　　A. None　　B. No one　　C. Nothing　　D. Nobody

(　　)21. This book is _____ mine.

　　A. as thicker as　　　　B. twice thicker than

　　C. two times thicker than　　D. twice thick of

(　　)22. _____ he lied to us is obvious.

　　A. What　　B. That　　C. Which　　D. Who

(　　)23. The temperature of Beijing is lower than _____ of Shanghai in winter.

　　A. that　　B. it　　C. one　　D. those

( )24. When I got to the station, the train _____.

　　A. leave　　　B. left　　　C. leaving　　　D. had left

( )25. She made a dress _____ the cloth her mother left her.

　　A. into　　　B. up　　　C. out of　　　D. from

( )26. We need a room _____ so we want to rent one.

　　A. to live　　　B. to live in　　　C. living　　　D. living in

( )27. They built a _____ wall to protect their country.

　　A. 100-meter-long　　　　　B. 100-meters-long

　　C. 100 meter long　　　　　D. 100 meters long

( )28. There is _____ in today's newspaper so you don't need to read it.

　　A. nothing serious　　　　　B. serious nothing

　　C. something serious　　　　D. serious something

( )29. I spent a whole week _____ the novel.

　　A. read　　　B. to read　　　C. reading　　　D. on reading

( )30. Don't ride too fast in the street _____ you will get hurt.

　　A. and　　　B. or　　　C. but　　　D. because

第三节　完形填空：阅读下面的短文，从所给的每组 A、B、C、D 四个选项中选择正确的答案，并在答题卡上将该项涂黑。（共 10 分，每小题 1 分）

　　The home computers industry has been growing rapidly in the United States for the last ten years. Computers ___31___ large, expensive machines that ___32___ very difficult to use.

　　But scientists and technicians have been making them smaller and ___33___ while at the same time they have been made easier ___34___. As a result, their popularity has been increasing as more people have been buying computers for their homes and businesses.

　　Computers have been designed to store information and compute complex problems.

　　Some have ___35___ that can speak with the operators. Stores use computers to keep records of their inventories(库存货物) and to send bills ___36___ their customers.

　　Offices use computers to type letters, record business and communicate ___37___ other offices.

　　People have been using computers in their homes to keep track of expenses and

116

turn appliances on and off.

One important new use for computers __38__ for entertainment. Many new games __39__ to be played on the computers. People of all ages have been playing these games. They have been going to shopping centers __40__ the computer games can be played for a small cost. People also have been buying home computers to play computer games at home. They have become very popular indeed.

( )31. A. used to be　　　　　　　　B. used to being
　　　　C. were used to be　　　　　D. were used to being

( )32. A. is　　　B. are　　　C. was　　　D. were

( )33. A. cheap　　B. cheaper　　C. more cheap　　D. cheapest

( )34. A. use　　B. used　　C. to use　　D. for use

( )35. A. voices　　B. sounds　　C. noises　　D. speeches

( )36. A. with　　B. for　　C. to　　D. of

( )37. A. for　　B. in　　C. to　　D. with

( )38. A. is　　B. are　　C. was　　D. were

( )39. A. have designed　　　　　　B. have been designed
　　　　C. has designed　　　　　　　D. has been designed

( )40. A. that　　B. which　　C. where　　D. when

第二部分　篇章与词汇理解

（共分三节，满分50分）

—— ★★★ ——

第一节　阅读理解：阅读下列短文，从每题所给A、B、C、D四个选项中，选出最恰当的答案，并在答题卡上将该项涂黑。（共30分，每小题2分）

A

One afternoon I toured an art museum while waiting for my husband to finish a business meeting. I was looking forward to a quiet view of the art works.

A young couple viewing the paintings ahead of me chatted non-stop between themselves. I watched them a moment and decided the wife was doing all the talk. I admired the husband's patience for putting up with her continuous talk. Distracted（心烦意乱）by their noise, I moved on.

I met them several times as I moved through the different rooms of art. Each time I heard her constant burst of words, I moved away quickly.

I was standing at the counter(柜台) of the museum gift shop making a purchase when the couple came near to the exit. Before they left, the man reached into his pocket and pulled out a white object. He extended it into a long stick and then tapped his way into the coatroom to get his wife's jacket.

"He's a brave man." The clerk at the counter said. "Most of us would give up if we were blinded at such a young age. During his recovery he made a promise that his life wouldn't change. So, as before, he and his wife come in whenever there's a new art show."

" But what does he get out of the art?" I asked. " He can't see."

"Can't see? You are wrong. He sees a lot. More than you or I do." the clerk said. "His wife describes each painting so he can see it in his head."

I learned something about patience, courage and love that day. I saw the patience of a young wife describing paintings to a person without sight and the courage of a husband who would not allow blindness to change his life. And I saw the love shared by two people as I watched this couple walk away hand in hand.

(　　)41. The young couple came to the art museum _____.

  A. to attend a meeting　　　　B. to appreciate art works

  C. to describe art shows　　　　D. to buy each painting

(　　)42. The writer moved away quickly because _____.

  A. she was in a hurry to buy some gifts

  B. she was tired of the non-stop talking

  C. she wasn't interested in the art show

  D. she was expecting to visit more rooms

(　　)43. We can infer from the passage that the husband _____.

  A. was not born blind　　　　B. couldn't understand his wife

  C. knew nothing about art　　　　D. completely depended on his wife

(　　)44. After hearing what the clerk had said about the couple, the writer was _____.

  A. excited　　　B. annoyed　　　C. moved　　　D. disappointed

(　　)45. The passage is mainly about _____.

　　A. the importance of art　　B. good manners in public

　　C. The patience of a husband　　D. the love between the couple

B

Hundreds of students send me emails each year for advice about education. They want to know what to study, or whether it's OK to drop out of college as what I did. A smaller number of parents send messages asking for suggestions for their sons or daughters. "How can we guide our child toward success?" they ask. My advice is simple, "Get the best education you can. Take advantage of high school and college. Learn how to learn."

It's true that I dropped out of college to start Microsoft, but I was at Harvard for three years before that. As I've said before, nobody should drop out of college unless they believe they face the chance of a lifetime. And even then they should consider carefully.

In our company's early years, quite a few people didn't finish college, but having a diploma certainly helps somebody who is looking for a job.

High school and college offer you the best chance to learn many things and to do projects with others that teach you about team spirit. In high school there was a time when I spent most of my time and energy on writing software, but for most of my high school years I had many interests. In college, I read about all kinds of things and attended different kinds of classes. For me classroom is not the only place where I can learn. You can also learn in a library. What's more, you should learn with other people, ask questions, try out ideas and have a way to test your ability. In a word, it's a real mistake not to take the chance to study a wide range of subjects and to learn to work with other people.

(　　)46. Every year a large number of _____ ask Bill Gates for advice about education.

　　A. teenagers　　B. sons or daughters

　　C. parents　　D. adults

(　　)47. Gates suggested young people _____ before stopping education.

　　A. learn how to learn　　B. think it over

　　C. ask for help　　D. make a careful plan

(　　)48. When Gates was in high school, he _____.

　　A. wrote nothing but software　　B. attended different kinds of classes

　　C. showed interest in many things　　D. read about all kinds of things

(　　)49. As a college student, Gates _____.

　　A. attended classes all day long

　　B. read all kinds of books about software

　　C. learnt all kinds of things in class

　　D. made full use of library

(　　)50. What did Gates value most in high school and college?

　　A. Visiting many places.

　　B. Writing software in spare time.

　　C. Developing interests and team spirit

　　D. Asking questions as many as possible.

C

　　Teachers often complain that students don't do their homework properly and that they are often arriving at school red-eyed and yawning(打哈欠) because of lack of sleep.

　　It appears that there are two main explanations for this phenomenon. Firstly, many young children stay up late to watch television. Progarmmes suitable for them should finish as late as seven o'clock. No child wants to be an exception at the same age of others and admit not having seen what everybody else has. Secondly, a growing number of older children, particularly those attending school are taking part in part-time jobs mainly involving evening or week-end work. They feel that working experience, not the knowledge learnt in the books, will help them find jobs after leaving school. One can agree with both groups of children but it doesn't make a teacher's life any easier.

(　　)51. What are teachers complaining about according to the passage?

　　A. Lack of disciplines of their students.

　　B. Their heavy work load.

　　C. Lack of understanding and support from students' parents.

　　D. Students' poor homework and laziness in study.

(　　)52. Why do the young children stay up late to watch television?

　　A. Because the programmes suitable for them finish late.

B. Because parents nowadays don't pay much attention to their children.

C. Because there isn't much homework for them to do.

D. Because good programmes start late.

( )53. How do part-time jobs affect school work?

A. Students often do their part-time jobs during the day.

B. part-time jobs have nothing to do with the students' school work.

C. part-time jobs take up less of study time.

D. Students usually feel exhausted after their part-time Jobs.

( )54. What is the author's attitude towards the two groups of school children?

A. He thinks they should be well guided.

B. He thinks they should be subject to strict disciplines.

C. He thinks they should be told how difficult their teacher's life is.

D. He thinks the students' behavior is understandable.

( )55. What is the passage mainly about?

A. Effect of TV programmes with school work.

B. Importance of working experience in job applications for school leaving students.

C. Causes of students' neglect of school work.

D. The hard life of the teachers.

第二节　词义搭配:从(B)栏中选出(A)栏单词的正确解释,并在答题卡上将该项涂黑。(共10分,每小题1分)

(A)	(B)
( )56. symbol	A. not likely to lie, cheat or steal
( )57. audience	B. to walk aimlessly
( )58. annoy	C. without words
( )59. nonverbal	D. of many different kinds
( )60. honest	E. established or well-known as a model of authority
( )61. wander	F. cause someone to be angry
( )62. collect	G. people who have gathered to hear or watch sb./sth.
( )63. various	H. of or relating to the mind
( )64. standard	I. get or bring together
( )65. mental	J. a sign, shape or object used to represent something else

第三节 补全对话:根据对话内容,从对话后的选项中选出能填入空白处的最佳选项,并在答题卡上将该项涂黑。(共10分,每小题2分)

A:You look unhappy today. __66__

B:Yesterday when I got home,I found my parents reading my diary. I've got very angry. Shouldn't I keep my own secrets?

A:Of course you can keep your secrets. __67__

B:No,but I shouted at them. They didn't say a word. They just kept silent. __68__

A:In fact,your parents shouldn't read your diary. They should respect your privacy. __69__ They want to make sure you aren't in any trouble,and they want to understand your life and study better in this way. Maybe you hurt your parents.

B:I agree. __70__

A:Say sorry to them. Try talking to them more. Let them know what you are doing,so that they won't worry about you so much.

B:OK,I will do as you told me.

> A. Did you quarrel with your parents?
> B. But your parents are just worried about you.
> C. That's a good idea.
> D. Now I feel very sad.
> E. What should I do now?
> F. What's the matter?
> G. I'm sorry to hear that.

第三部分 语言技能运用

(共分四节,满分30分)

———★★★———

第一节 单词拼写:根据下列句子及所给汉语注释,在答题卡上相应题号后的横线上写出该单词。(共5分,每小题1分)

71. If you _____ (不同意) with my views,can you give me an explanation?

72. We communicate with each other by _____ (方法) of words and body language.

73. Don't feel _____ (沮丧的) when we fail in anything.

74. Our _____ (知识) and experience increase with ages.

75. Success needs efforts and _____ (耐心).

第二节 词形变换:用括号内单词的适当形式填空,将正确答案写在答题卡上相应题号后的横线上。(共5分,每小题1分)

76. The actress was so _____ (attract) that we were all deeply involved in the movie.

77. It became _____ (fashion) to eat certain kinds of fish.

78. No one wants to be _____ (understand) by others.

79. Yesterday we met several _____ (foreign) and we had a conversation with them.

80. _____ (consider) the working conditions, the boss increased the salary for us.

第三节 改错:从 A、B、C、D 四个画线处找出一处错误的选项填入答题卡上相应题号后的括号内,并在横线上写出正确答案。(共10分,每小题2分)

81. Following the road and you will find the house.
     A   B   C   D

82. I think that impossible to finish the work in five days.
  A   B   C   D

83. He was praised because what he did in the big fire.
    A   B   C   D

84. He always says nothing but give us a lot of help when we are in trouble.
            A   B   C   D

85. The number of tourists come to visit the Summer Palace every year.
    A   B   C   D

81. ( ) 应为_____   82. ( ) 应为_____

83. ( ) 应为_____   84. ( ) 应为_____

85. ( ) 应为_____

第四节 书面表达。(共10分)

作文题目:On-line Voting(网上投票)。

词数要求:80~100 词。

写作要点:1. 结合当下流行的网络投票,谈谈自己对网上投票的看法。

2. 参考词汇:opportunities,convenient,fairness,feedback(反馈)。

综合模拟试题(四)

第一部分 英语知识运用

（共分三节，满分40分）

★★★

第一节 语音知识：从 A、B、C、D 四个选项中找出其画线部分与所给单词画线部分读音相同的选项，并在答题卡上将该项涂黑。（共5分，每小题1分）

( ) 1. extra　　　A. expert　　　B. express　　　C. extend　　　D. excel

( ) 2. contest　　A. concern　　B. educate　　　C. official　　　D. notice

( ) 3. earn　　　A. wear　　　B. appear　　　C. hear　　　　D. research

( ) 4. south　　　A. trousers　　B. touch　　　　C. trouble　　　D. nervous

( ) 5. plays　　　A. speaks　　　B. follows　　　C. thinks　　　D. likes

第二节 词汇与语法知识：从 A、B、C、D 四个选项中选出可以填入空白处的最佳选项，并在答题卡上将该项涂黑。（共25分，每小题1分）

( ) 6. I saw _____ one-eyed sheep walked by _____ 11-year-old boy.
　　A. the, a　　　B. an, the　　　C. a, an　　　　D. an, a

( ) 7. She caught me _____ and smiled happily.
　　A. by my arm　　　　　　　　　B. in my arm
　　C. by the arm　　　　　　　　　D. in the arm

( ) 8. I always talk with the boy, _____ mother is a teacher.
　　A. who　　　B. whose　　　C. whom　　　D. which

( ) 9. No sooner _____ back home _____ his cellphone began to ring.
　　A. had the boy come, when　　　B. had the boy come, than
　　C. did the boy come, when　　　D. did the boy come, than

( ) 10. He served in the army in _____.
　　A. 1980's　　B. the 1980's　　C. his 1980　　D. his 1980's

( ) 11. John, together with his sisters, _____ to the party.

124

A. has invited   B. has been invited
C. have invited   D. have been invited

( )12. —You put your coat outside last night.
　　—Oh,my God! _____.
　　A. So did I   B. So I did   C. Nor did I   D. Nor I did

( )13. He ordered that the work _____ in five minutes.
　　A. finished   B. should finish   C. be finished   D. would be finished

( )14. He did nothing but _____ a letter to his brother.
　　A. writing   B. to write   C. write   D. be writing

( )15. Our office is too dirty. It needs _____.
　　A. clean   B. to clean   C. cleaned   D. cleaning

( )16. This is one of the most exciting football matches _____ I have ever watched.
　　A. which   B. when   C. of which   D. that

( )17. The police are searching a boy _____ Tom.
　　A. named   B. naming   C. to name   D. being named

( )18. _____ I can't understand is _____ he said such words at the meeting.
　　A. What,why   B. What,that   C. That,what   D. That,why

( )19. He told his mother what he _____ on the way to school.
　　A. see   B. had seen   C. saw   D. was seeing

( )20. _____ number of people going to visit the park hasn't been known.
　　A. A   B. The   C. An   D. /

( )21. The boys dislike the old museum, _____ they?
　　A. do   B. don't   C. are   D. aren't

( )22. Can you see a woman and her horse _____ are crossing the bridge?
　　A. which   B. that   C. who   D. whom

( )23. It _____ me five days _____ the task.
　　A. took,to finish   B. took,finishing
　　C. spent,finishing   D. spent,on finishing

( )24. It _____ last night because the ground is wet.
　　A. must rain   B. must have rained
　　C. may rain   D. can't have rained

( )25. He is the only one of the teachers _____ French in our school.
　　A. who teach   B. who teaches   C. which teach   D. which teaches

( )26. It was _____ good advice that all of us agreed to it.
    A. so   B. such   C. so a   D. such a

( )27. Don't leave the door _____ when you are sleeping.
    A. open   B. opened   C. opening   D. to open

( )28. _____ in many countries, he has seen many beautiful sceneries.
    A. Travelling   B. Travelled   C. To travel   D. Being travelled

( )29. _____ of us has an English dictionary.
    A. Each   B. Every   C. Each one   D. Everyone

( )30. He does things _____ us.
    A. different from   B. differently from
    C. differs from   D. difference from

第三节　完形填空：阅读下面的短文，从所给的每组 A、B、C、D 四个选项中选择正确的答案，并在答题卡上将该项涂黑。（共 10 分，每小题 1 分）

    Education in the United States is usually divided __31__ four levels. These are early childhood, elementary, secondary and higher education. School attendance is required in every state of the country, and in most states students must attend school __32__ the age of 16.

    __33__ first level is early childhood education. Its main purpose is to prepare children for school.

    The second level is elementary education. Education at this level is divided into six or eight grades and children learn Reading, Arithmetic, Writing, Social Studies __34__ Science. They __35__ have Art, Music and Physical Education.

    The __36__ level is secondary education. It is for junior and senior high school students. Some students take courses to prepare __37__ for college. Other students take technical or vocational courses that __38__ them for jobs after they graduate from high school.

    Higher education continues __39__ high school. There are many kinds of institutions of higher education. Technical institutes offer __40__ programmes in Electronics, Engineering, Business and other subjects. After two years at a junior college, students receive an associate degree and then they can continue at a four-year college.

( )31. A. at   B. into   C. from   D. with

( )32. A. from   B. into   C. until   D. since

( )33. A. The   B. A   C. An   D. /

( )34. A. and B. or C. but D. except

( )35. A. too B. also C. either D. as well

( )36. A. third B. three C. threeth D. thirdth

( )37. A. they B. themself C. themselves D. their

( )38. A. prepare B. prepares C. is preparing D. are preparing

( )39. A. before B. after C. since D. during

( )40. A. two year's B. two years C. two-year D. two-years

第二部分　篇章与词汇理解

（共分三节，满分50分）

——★★★——

第一节　阅读理解：阅读下列短文，从每题所给A、B、C、D四个选项中，选出最恰当的答案，并在答题卡上将该项涂黑。（共30分，每小题2分）

A

The designer of Apple Computer, Steve Jobs, was not quite successful in his early years. He was not among the best students at school. And from time to time he got into trouble with either his classmates or his teachers. But he was full of new ideas, which few people saw the value of. Things remained the same when he went up to college, and he dropped out half way.

Steve Jobs worked first as a video game designer at Atari. He worked for only a few months and then he began to tour India. He hoped that the trip would give him more ideas and give him a change in life for the better.

After he had returned from India, he lived on a farm in California. And then, in 1975, Steve Jobs started making a new type of computer. Along with his friend Steven Wozniak, he designed the Apple I computer in his bedroom and really built it in his garage. He chose the name "Apple" because it caused him to think of a happy summer he once spent on an orchard(果园) in Oregon.

His Apple computer was such a great success in the end that Steve Jobs soon became worldwide famous.

( )41. When Steve Jobs studied at school he _____.

A. was one of the best students

B. was getting on well with his teachers

C. was not considered as one of the best students

D. study hard and was full of new ideas

( )42. The underlined word "tour" in the second paragraph means _____.
   A. study   B. look for
   C. discover   D. make a journey round

( )43. What did Steve Jobs work first as at Atari?
   A. A video game designer.   B. A teacher.
   C. A computer expert.   D. A waiter.

( )44. When he began to design and build the Apple I computer _____.
   A. no one helped him   B. he had a lot of money
   C. his working conditions were poor   D. He was famous enough

( )45. Why did Steve Jobs name the computer "Apple"?
   A. He likes to eat apples.
   B. He wanted to memorize a friend.
   C. Because the computer was built in a orchard.
   D. Apple reminds him of a summer he spent.

B

On October 12, 2005, China launched its second manned spaceship, Shenzhou VI, sending two spacemen into space. It was the second time that our country had sent up manned spaceship after Shenzhou V. China has become the third country to send people to space after Russia and the USA.

Shenzhou VI lifted off on a Long March 2F rocket from Jiuquan, Gansu Province. Two spacemen Fei Junlong and Nie Haisheng travelled around the earth 80 times in 115 hours and thirty-two minutes and landed safely in the Inner Mongolian grasslands on October 17, 2005.

The spaceship has three modules(飞船舱): The orbital module where scientific experiments like testing space foods and drinks are done, the re-entry capsule where the spacemen spent most of their time and the service module, which has fuel(燃料), air and other technical equipment(技术设备) in it.

Unlike Yang Liwei's space trip six years ago, Fei and Nie went up and down between the modules for scientific experiments. For the first time they took off their space suits and moved around in the modules freely. From space, Fei and Nie could make long distance calls to their families at the launch centre. Nie's daughter even sang "Happy Birthday" to her dad during the phone call.

( )46. The spacemen Fei and Nie travelled around the earth for nearly _____ days.
   A. four   B. five   C. six   D. seven

(　　)47. We can infer that Fei Junlong and Nie Haisheng had foods and drinks in _____.

A. the orbital module　　　B. the re-entry capsule

C. the service module　　　D. the launch centre

(　　)48. Which statement is NOT right according to the passage?

A. Shenzhou Ⅵ was sent up into space in Gansu Province

B. The re-entry capsule has fuel and air in it.

C. Nie Haisheng spent his birthday in the spaceship.

D. China will probably walk in space one day.

(　　)49. Which of the following orders is right?

①The spacemen took off their space suits and moved around in the modules.

②Shenzhou Ⅵ landed in the Inner Mongolian grasslands.

③A Long March 2F rocket was sent up into space.

④Shenzhou Ⅴ was sent up.

A. ④③①②　　B. ③①④②　　C. ③④②①　　D. ④③②①

(　　)50. This passage maybe comes from _____.

A. a magazine　　B. a story book　　C. a newspaper　　D. an advertisement

C

We were on a tour a few summers ago, driving through Chicago and when right outside the city, we got pulled over. A middle-aged policeman came up to the car and was really being troublesome at first. Lecturing us, he said, "You were speeding. Where are you going in such a hurry?" Our guitarist, Tim, told him that we were on our way to Wisconsin to play a show. His way towards us totally changed. He asked, "Oh, so you boys are in a band (乐队)?" We told him that we were. He then asked all the usual band questions about the type of music we played, and how long we had been at it.

Suddenly, he stopped and said, "Tim, you want to get out of this ticket, don't you?" Tim said, "Yes." So the officer asked him to step out of the car. The rest of us, inside the car, didn't know what to think as we watched the policeman talk to Tim. Next thing we knew, the policeman was putting Tim in the back of the police car he had parked in front of us. With that, he threw the car into reverse(倒车), stopping a few feet in back of our car. Now we suddenly felt frightened. We didn't know if we were all going to prison, or if the policeman was going to sell Tim on the black market or something.

All of a sudden, the policeman's voice came over his loudspeaker. He said, "Ladies and gentlemen, for the first time ever, we have Tim here singing on Route 90." Turns out, the policeman had told Tim that the only way he was getting out of the ticket was if he sang part of one of our songs over the loudspeaker in the police car. Seconds later, Tim started screaming into the receiver. The policeman enjoyed the performance, and sent us on our way without a ticket.

(　　)51. The policeman stopped the boys to _____.

　　A. put them into prison　　　　B. give them a ticket

　　C. ask some band questions　　D. enjoy their performance

(　　)52. The policeman became friendly to the boys when he knew they _____.

　　A. played the music he loved　　B. had long been at the band

　　C. were driving for a show　　　D. promised him a performance

(　　)53. The boys probably felt _____ when they drove off.

　　A. joyful　　　B. calm　　　C. nervous　　　D. frightened

(　　)54. Which is Not true according to the passage?

　　A. A policeman stopped us when we were driving.

　　B. The policeman put Tim in the back of the police car and sold him on the black market.

　　C. The policeman asked Tim to sing part of one of our songs over the loudspeaker in the police car.

　　D. We were not fined at last.

(　　)55. Which is the best title of the passage?

　　A. A Wonderful Tour.　　　　　B. A Wonderful Performance.

　　C. A Pleasant Surprise.　　　　D. A Beautiful Song.

第二节　词义搭配:从(B)栏中选出(A)栏单词的正确解释,并在答题卡上将该项涂黑。(共10分,每小题1分)

　　　(A)　　　　　　　　　　　(B)

(　　)56. edge　　　　　　　A. usual daily food and drink

(　　)57. diet　　　　　　　　B. of the present time

(　　)58. grammar　　　　　C. a person related by blood or marriage

(　　)59. modern　　　　　　D. give an appearance of sth. that is not true

(　　)60. relative　　　　　　E. make something dirty

(　　)61. pollute　　　　　　F. the line where something ends or begins

(　　)62. expect　　　　　　G. think or believe that something will happen

(　　)63. normal　　　　　　H. make or produce on a large scale by machinery

(　　)64. manufacture　　　I. usual or average

(　　)65. pretend　　　　　　J. the principles that govern the words of a language

第三节 补全对话:根据对话内容,从对话后的选项中选出能填入空白处的最佳选项,并在答题卡上将该项涂黑。(共10分,每小题2分)

A:Hi,Henry. Haven't seen you for ages. Where have you been?

B:I have been in hospital.

A:I am sorry to hear that. __66__

B:Oh,I had a car accident two weeks ago.

A:Really? __67__

B:Yes. But luckily,only my left arm was broken. And I can move it now.

A:Good. __68__

B:I was driving on the Broad Street and knocked into a pole.

A: __69__

B:Yes,and I regret doing that.

A:Remember the lesson. __70__

B:Thanks a lot.

> A. But how did that happen?
> B. Is it true?
> C. But what for?
> D. How are you feeling now?
> E. I wish you could return to work soon.
> F. So you were injured and had to be treated in hospital.
> G. You drove too fast,I suppose.

第三部分 语言技能运用

(共分四节,满分30分)

——★★★——

第一节 单词拼写:根据下列句子及所给汉语注释,在答题卡上相应题号后的横线上写出该单词。(共5分,每小题1分)

71. Have you considered _____(选择)jeans instead of a dress?

72. Mobile phones are _____ (广泛地) used in many fields.

73. The restaurant is famous for its good _____(服务).

74. A good education is helpful to _____(成功)and independence.

75. Tickets are available on _____(申请).

第二节 词形变换：用括号内单词的适当形式填空，将正确答案写在答题卡上相应题号后的横线上。（共 5 分，每小题 1 分）

76. The word "blue" is _____ (interest) connected with the stock market.

77. Judging from his _____ (face) expression, he is not satisfied with my words.

78. Don't say anything in _____ (angry) and try to control your temper.

79. My mother had my family photo _____ (large) and put on the wall.

80. _____ (cover) with fallen leaves, the road looks more beautiful.

第三节 改错：从 A、B、C、D 四个画线处找出一处错误的选项填入答题卡上相应题号后的括号内，并在横线上写出正确答案。（共 10 分，每小题 2 分）

81. Tom is one of the boys who has been to America.
    A B C   D

82. I feel that nervous to talk with others in English.
   A B   C   D

83. I wish I helped you when the accident happened.
  A B   C   D

84. The meeting held now is about how to protect our environment.
     A   B C   D

85. He has never gone abroad ago.
  A B C   D

81.（　　）应为_____　　82.（　　）应为_____

83.（　　）应为_____　　84.（　　）应为_____

85.（　　）应为_____

第四节 书面表达。（共 10 分）

作文题目：My View on Opportunity。

词数要求：80～100 词。

写作要点：1. 不同人对于机会有不同的看法，有些人认为机会是有限的，有些人认为每个人都有自己的机会。

     2. 请你针对机会发表自己的看法。

参考答案

Unit 1 Social Communication

单元基础知识闯关小测验

Ⅰ. 汉译英。

1. be tolerant of   2. have some / no trouble in doing sth.   3. be annoyed with
4. leave out   5. pretend to do   6. talk with   7. switch to   8. explain sth. to sb.

Ⅱ. 词形变换。

1. tolerance   2. explanation   3. polite   4. loss   5. misunderstand   6. facial

Ⅲ. 用括号内所给词的适当形式填空。

1. response   2. misunderstood   3. Child   4. standing   5. left   6. annoyed

单元综合练习

第一节 1～5 CCCDB

第二节 1～5 BCBCD   6～10 CDDCA   11～15 DBDAA   16～20 DCBDC

第三节 1～5 BCAAB   6～10 AACDC

第四节 1～5 BADCA

第五节 1～5 CDAEB

第六节 1～5 BDCEA

第七节 1. disagree   2. explain   3. switched   4. compliment   5. misunderstood

第八节 1. difficulty   2. politely   3. friendship   4. suitable   5. means

第九节 1. C 应为 sending / to be sent   2. A 应为 What   3. C 应为 standing
4. B 应为 to call   5. D 应为 left out

第十节 略

Unit 2 Making Choices in Life

单元基础知识闯关小测验

Ⅰ. 汉译英。

1. turn to sb. for help   2. be involved in   3. thanks to   4. insist on

133

5. look around   6. light up   7. pay for   8. argue \ quarrel with

Ⅱ. 词形变换。

1. choice   2. success   3. honestly   4. full   5. stomachs   6. attractive

Ⅲ. 用括号内所给词的适当形式填空。

1. depressed   2. stomachs   3. treatment   4. am   5. passing   6. honestly

单元综合练习

第一节 1～5 ACCBD

第二节 1～5 CDBCC   6～10 BABAA   11～15 BDBCD   16～20 DBCBA

第三节 1～5 DCADC   6～10 BBCBC

第四节 1～5 DADBD

第五节 1～5 BEACD

第六节 1～5 FGBEC

第七节 1. clerks   2. attracted   3. depressed   4. upstairs   5. choices

第八节 1. argument 2. successfully 3. happiness   4. amazing   5. death

第九节 1. C 应为 finished   2. C 应为 knows   3. D 应为 she should do   4. D 应为 she
        5. A 应为 used to

第十节 略

阶段测试题（Unit 1～Unit 2）

第一部分　英语知识运用

第一节 1～5 BBCAD

第二节 6～10 BCBCD   11～15 BACCC   16～20 CAAAB   21～25 CBCCA
        26～30 DCBCC

第三节 31～35 ACBDA   36～40 CDCBA

第二部分　篇章与词汇理解

第一节 41～45 CCCDD   46～50 DBACB   51～55 ABCDC

第二节 56～65 CEGJH   FAIDB

第三节 66～70 BEACD

第三部分　语言技能运用

第一节 71. gestures   72. suitable   73. attracts   74. tireless   75. injured

第二节 76. expression   77. lively   78. successfully   79. decision   80. misunderstood

第三节　81. C 应为 knows　82. C 应为 is　83. B 应为 buying　84. C 应为 taking

85. D 应为 she would

第四节　参考范文：

How to Be Successful

What is success? Different people have different opinions. As a businessman, his success is making a great deal of money. As a teacher, his success is to send his students to go to university to study. As a doctor, his success is to see his patients become healthy again.

As a student, if I can go to university to study, it will be a kind of success to me. "No pain, no gain." Without hard work, no one can be successful. So I must work hard every day to make progress. In this way can I fulfill my dream and be successful.

Unit 3 Fashion

单元基础知识闯关小测验

Ⅰ. 汉译英。

1. step into　2. put on　3. lie down　4. wear out　5. a piece of history　6. in a word

7. make...into　8. keep down

Ⅱ. 词形变换。

1. uncomfortable　2. France　3. gradually　4. vary　5. strengthen　6. fashionable

Ⅲ. 用括号内所给词的适当形式填空。

1. interesting, interested　2. sitting　3. being built　4. followed　5. heard

6. Hearing

单元综合练习

第一节　1~5 ABDDA

第二节　1~5 BADDC　6~10 CBACA　11~15 ADBCA　16~20 BDABD

第三节　1~5 CACAD　6~10 CBCAC

第四节　1~5 BCBCB

第五节　1~5 BEDAC

第六节　1~5 ECDAB

第七节　1. manufactured　2. rainbow　3. priced　4. available　5. suitable

第八节　1. following　2. built　3. strengthen　4. uncomfortable　5. fashionable

第九节　1. A 应为 Having watered　2. D 应为 dyed　3. A 应为 closely　4. C 应为 are

　　　　5. B 应为 to strengthen

第十节　略

Unit 4 Colors and Mood

单元基础知识闯关小测验

Ⅰ. 汉译英。

　1. be fined for　2. under the control of　3. shift from...to...　4. refer to

　5. be in low spirits　6. believe it or not　7. warn...of...　8. see red

Ⅱ. 词形变换。

　1. unpleasant　2. association　3. policemen　4. connect　5. affect　6. choosy

Ⅲ. 选择正确答案。

　1～6　CBBDCD

单元综合练习

第一节　1～5　ADDBA

第二节　1～5　AADBC　6～10　CBACA　11～15　CDBCA　16～20　BDACD

第三节　1～5　BDAAC　6～10　BADCB

第四节　1～5　ABBAD

第五节　1～5　ECABD

第六节　1～5　ECABD

第七节　1. impression　2. nervous　3. scientific　4. association　5. bruises

第八节　1. connection　2. application　3. eases　4. Calming　5. decorated

第九节　1. A 应为 why　2. B 应为 under　3. B 应为 going

　　　　4. A 应为 Having Failed　5. D 应为 a bad

第十节　略

阶段测试题（Unit 3～Unit 4）

第一部分　英语知识运用

第一节　1～5　DCABC

第二节　6～10　ACBDA　11～15　CDCCD　16～20　BACBD　21～25　BCADC

　　　　26～30　BABCB

第三节　31~35 CABDA　36~40 BDBBC

第二部分　篇章与词汇理解

第一节　41~45 DBCBA　46~50 BBBDC　51~55 CABCB

第二节　56~65 BFHGADEJCI

第三节　66~70 EACDB

第三部分　语言技能运用

第一节　71. optimistic　72. restaurants　73. standard　74. interestingly　75. decorating

第二节　76. speaking　77. unpleasant　78. joy　79. ease　80. treatment

第三节　81. A 应为 as　82. A 应为 On　83. D 应为 hasn't he　84. C 应为 with

85. D 应为 for

第四节　参考范文：

What Is Most Important?

What is most important in our life? Different people have different answers. Some students believe money is important. With enough money, they can buy whatever they want. Some students think being in good health is of great importance and others believe friendship is valuable in their lives.

I don't fully agree with the views above. We can't buy everything important with money, such as health, happiness and knowledge, which are valuable for us. I value knowledge, which makes me happy and I can do much for mankind with knowledge.

Although different people think differently, what I value most in my life is knowledge.

Unit 5　Good Manners

单元基础知识闯关小测验

Ⅰ.汉译英。

1. be familiar with　2. in daily life　3. lose one's temper　4. be/feel ashamed of

5. regret doing...　6. apologize for　7. in other words　8. no longer

Ⅱ.词形变换。

1. inconvenience　2. understand　3. apology　4. employ　5. similar　6. often

Ⅲ.用 one, none, few, a few, little, a little 填空。

1. none　2. a few　3. a little　4. few; one　5. little

单元综合练习

第一节 1～5 DBADA

第二节 1～5 DCABA 6～10 CCDAA 11～15 DBCAB 16～20 ABCDD

第三节 1～5 DABCB 6～10 DACAC

第四节 1～5 BDCDA

第五节 1～5 ECADB

第六节 1～5 CEADB

第七节 1. ashamed 2. chance 3. doubt 4. making 5. recognized

第八节 1. understandable 2. inconvenience 3. strengthened 4. damaged
         5. apology

第九节 1. B 应为 dressed 2. A 应为 Having 3. B 应为 arguing 4. D 应为 to finish
         5. C 应为 big

第十节 略

Unit 6 Chinese Heritage

单元基础知识闯关小测验

Ⅰ.汉译英。

　　1. originate in 2. be characterized by… 3. date back to/from 4. in common with
　　5. by the order of 6. be accompanied by 7. consist of… 8. correspond to…

Ⅱ.词形变换。

　　1. performer/performance 2. combination 3. musical 4. characterize
　　5. humorous 6. indicate

Ⅲ.用括号中词的适当形式填空。

　　1. to pass 2. laughing 3. to read 4. turning 5. trying 6. speaking

单元综合练习

第一节 1～5 DBACA

第二节 1～5 CCCAB 6～10 ACDCA 11～15 BBBAD 16～20 CBDAB

第三节 1～5 DBABA 6～10 CDBAC

第四节 1～5 CADCB

第五节 1～5 EDABC

第六节 1～5 EABCD

第七节　1. culture　2. stage　3. attractive　4. Traditional　5. balance

第八节　1. Medical　2. dependent　3. readjust　4. humorous　5. importance

第九节　1. B 应为 avoid　2. B 应为 to give　3. D 应为 playing　4. D 应为 roles
　　　　5. A 应为 Symbolism

第十节　略

阶段测试题（Unit 5～Unit 6）

第一部分　英语知识运用

第一节　1～5 DBACA

第二节　6～10 BDABC　11～15 ADADB　16～20 CCABD　21～25 ADBCA
　　　　26～30 ADBBD

第三节　31～35 CBDCA　36～40 CBDAA

第二部分　篇章与词汇理解

第一节　41～45 CADBD　46～50 ABACD　51～55 DCBAA

第二节　56～65 JDIGEACBFH

第三节　66～70 DCAEB

第三部分　语言技能运用

第一节　71. apology　72. communication　73. accept　74. traditional　75. regret

第二节　76. expression　77. succeeded　78. friendly　79. employee　80. available

第三节　81. D 应为 repaired　82. C 应为 can you　83. C 应为 to show　84. B 应为 for
　　　　85. A 应为 Learning

第四节　参考范文：

The Great Changes in My Hometown

With the development of economy, great changes have taken place in my hometown.

My hometown lies in the mountains. It used to be very poor, but now it is changing into a beautiful countryside. A new highway to the big cities is through my village like a white belt. A new school is being built behind the old one. Many new bikes, motorbikes even new cars are seen in the village. Another hospital has been built nearby. All the mountains are covered by green trees and grass. But a few years ago, the mountains here were bare, and the villagers had not enough to eat.

What great changes we have had in my hometown! Now my hometown looks like a newly born boy to grow up on its way.

期中测试题

第一部分 英语知识运用

第一节　1～5 DABCA

第二节　6～10 CBCCB　11～15 DDACD　16～20 DADBA　21～25 CBCBD

26～30 ABACB

第三节　31～35 CABDA　36～40 BBCDA

第二部分 篇章与词汇理解

第一节　41～45 ADCAD　46～50 CDBBC　51～55 BCCCB

第二节　56～65 FCEBGIAJDH

第三节　66～70 CDEAB

第三部分 语言技能运用

第一节　71. explain　72. succeeded　73. various　74. carefree　75. fashion

第二节　76. politely　77. strengthen　78. happily　79. native　80. depressed

第三节　81. D 应为 not to see　82. D 应为 didn't he　83. A 应为 to the workers

84. B 应为 had helped　85. A 应为 were sold out/sold well

第四节　参考范文：

Attitude Towards Life

Life is a long journey for everyone. And attitude plays an important part in the journey of life.

People like to say being happy is a day, being unhappy is also a day. Why not choose an optimistic attitude and live happily? So my attitude towards life is being happy every day. Only when we are happy, can we work effectively. After finishing the work or task, we can enjoy the life. Moreover being happy can make other people happy, and you can make friends easily.

期末测试题

第一部分 英语知识运用

第一节　1～5 DBCAB

第二节　6～10 CBAAC　11～15 BDDBA　16～20 BCBBD　21～25 ABCAC

26～30 DDBAC

第三节　31～35 CDABA　36～40 CDBBA

第二部分　篇章与词汇理解

第一节　41～45 ADDCB　46～50 ACACD　51～55 ADCAD

第二节　56～65 DIGBCAEJFH

第三节　66～70 DEAFB

第三部分　语言技能运用

第一节　71. choices　72. rude　73. decision　74. shape　75. temper

第二节　76. Generally　77. marked　78. honestly　79. successful　80. various

第三节　81. C 应为 to　82. C 应为 to　83. A 应为 It　84. C 应为 can we

85. C 去掉 but

第四节　参考范文：

The Mobile Phones at School

More and more students like to carry mobile phones to school even to their class. It has become a problem for middle schools.

Mobile phone use is a distraction to students in class and it also gives teachers so much trouble in their classrooms. Teachers are also saying that sometimes students might use phone messages to cheat during exams. Besides, it is a waste of time and money for students to overuse phones.

In order to make students study hard and grow healthily, mobile phones should be forbidden to be carried to school during school hours.

综合模拟试题（一）

第一部分　英语知识运用

第一节　1～5 CABBD

第二节　6～10 BACCC　11～15 DBCCD　16～20 ABCCB　21～25 CDCBA
　　　　26～30 DCCCB

第三节　31～35 DDAAB　36～40 BCBCD

第二部分　篇章与词汇理解

第一节　41～45 CBCCA　46～50 CBCDD　51～55 ACDDA

第二节　56～65 DEBGHACJFI

第三节　66～70 CABDE

第三部分　语言技能运用

第一节　71. confidence　72. application　73. choice　74. mislead　75. support

第二节　76. length　77. flying　78. Unluckily　79. feeling　80. Germans

第三节　81. A 应为 What　82. A 应为 Having been told　83. D 应为 however

84. B 应为 great progress　85. B 应为 crying

第四节　参考范文：

Our Life in the future

What will our life be like in the future? I think it will be better and better. The transportation will become cleaner, faster and safer. Cars will be controlled by computer. With the development of medicine, the way diseases are treated will be changed and genes may be used as a cure. Distance education will help people study whenever they have time and wherever they may be, so it will be more convenient for personal study. As for business, online shopping will become more and more popular. People may also go to a mall which combines shopping with fun.

In a word, our future life will become more and more colorful.

综合模拟试题（二）

第一部分　英语知识运用

第一节　1～5 BDCDA

第二节　6～10 CABBC　11～15 DAACB　16～20 CAABD　21～25 BDABA

26～30 BAACB

第三节　31～35 BBDAC　36～40 BDDBA

第二部分　篇章与词汇理解

第一节　41～45 ABDDB　46～50 ADABB　51～55 CBDCC

第二节　56～65 BFHAJDEICG

第三节　66～70 DFACE

第三部分　语言技能运用

第一节　71. published　72. selfish　73. challenging　74. traditional　75. colorful

第二节　76. importance　77. facial　78. apology　79. Unluckily　80. management

第三节　81. B 应为 where　82. B 应为 as tall as　83. C 应为 that　84. C 应为 on

85. A 应为 It

第四节　参考范文：

The Advantages and Disadvantages of Studying Abroad

Nowadays many middle school students would like to study abroad, because they think it may affect their work and life in the future.

The following is the advantages of studying abroad: First, it gives them a good environment of language study. Second, they can learn the advanced science and technology of other countries. At the same time, they can also spread our national culture to foreign countries.

The negative aspects are also clear. The middle school students are too young to look after themselves and they are short of life experience. And the cost for their life and study is too high.

Therefore, parents and children should consider their conditions and make a reasonable decision. As for me, I prefer to go abroad for my further education.

综合模拟试题(三)

第一部分 英语知识运用

第一节　1～5 ABDCB

第二节　6～10 CCBCC　11～15 CDCCA　16～20 CDABA　21～25 BBADC
　　　　26～30 BAACB

第三节　31～35 ADBCA　36～40 CDABC

第二部分 篇章与词汇理解

第一节　41～45 BBACD　46～50 AACDC　51～55 DADDC

第二节　56～65 JGFCABIDEH

第三节　66～70 FADBE

第三部分 语言技能运用

第一节　71. disagree　72. means　73. depressed　74. knowledge　75. patience

第二节　76. attractive　77. fashionable　78. misunderstood　79. foreigners
　　　　80. considering

第三节　81. A 应为 Follow　82. B 应为 it　83. B 应为 because of　84. B 应为 to give
　　　　85. A 应为 A

第四节　参考范文：

On-line Voting

With the development of the Internet, on-line voting has become more and more popular. Some people think it is convenient and rapid, while others think personal emotions may affect the fairness.

In my opinion, on-line voting is good. First, lots of people now get involved in many competitions and they need votes to win the game. On-line voting can offer people more opportunities to take part in a variety of social activities without much effort. Second, people don't need to waste too much time or money and can vote the person they like best through computer or cellphone. Voting on the Internet makes instant feedback possible.

So I hold a positive attitude to on-line voting.

综合模拟试题(四)

第一部分　英语知识运用

第一节　1~5 ABDAB

第二节　6~10 CCBBB　11~15 BBCCD　16~20 DAABB　21~25 BBABB
　　　　26~30 BAAAB

第三节　31~35 BCAAB　36~40 ACABC

第二部分　篇章与词汇理解

第一节　41~45 CDACD　46~50 BBBAC　51~55 BCABC

第二节　56~65 FAJBCEGIHD

第三节　66~70 CFAGE

第三部分　语言技能运用

第一节　71. choosing　72. widely　73. service　74. success　75. application

第二节　76. interestingly　77. facial　78. anger　79. enlarged　80. Covered

第三节　81. D 应为 have been　82. A 应为 it　83. B 应为 had helped
　　　　84. A 应为 being held　85. D 应为 before

第四节　参考范文：

My View on Opportunity

Different people have different views on opportunity. Some people think that the opportunity for everyone is limited, while others think that there are many opportunities in our life.

As for me, I believe opportunities are everywhere around us. Everyone will be lucky enough to meet his own opportunity. But we have to make good preparation and improve ourselves. So when opportunities are coming, we can catch them and make full use of them. In a word, we should get prepared for our opportunities instead of letting them pass by.